The Grid and the Village

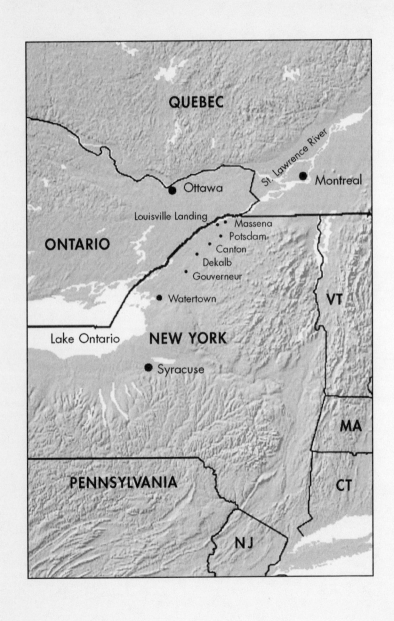

The Grid and the Village   Stephen Doheny-Farina

losing electricity, finding community, surviving disaster

Yale University Press   New Haven and London

for the volunteers

Photo credits: National Weather Service Historical Photo Collection, National Oceanic and Atmospheric Administration, Department of Commerce (pp. xiv, 114); New York State Emergency Management Office, photo by Dennis Michalski (pp. 24, 156); FEMA News Photo, Federal Emergency Management Agency, photo by New York State Electric and Gas (pp. 56, 188); FEMA News Photo, Federal Emergency Management Agency, photo by Sandra Thornton (pp. 86, 196).

Designed by Sonia Shannon.
Set in Bembo and Futura types by dix! Syracuse, New York.
Printed in the United States of America by R. R. Donnelley & Sons, Harrisonburg, Virginia.

Library of Congress Cataloging-in-Publication Data
Doheny-Farina, Stephen.
   The grid and the village : losing electricity, finding community, surviving disaster / Stephen Doheny-Farina.
p.   cm.
Includes bibliographical references and index.
   ISBN 0-300-08977-5 (alk. paper)
   1. Electric power distribution—New York (State)—Cold weather conditions.   2. Electric power failures—New York (State)—Potsdam Region—Social aspects—Case studies.   3. Ice storms—New York (State)—Saint Lawrence County—History.   4. Potsdam Region (N.Y.)—Social life and customs—20th century.   I. Title.
TK3091.D56   2001
363.34'92—dc21   2001000355

A catalogue record for this book is available from the British Library.
The paper in this book meets the guidelines for permanence and durability of the Committee on Production Guidelines for Book Longevity of the Council on Library Resources.

10 9 8 7 6 5 4 3 2 1

102

contents

Y ou know, I lived through a tornado once."
"Really?"
"Yes sir. Downstate. I also saw a big flood up close when I was a trooper in Corning. It must have been the early seventies sometime. Hurricane Agnes."
"Hey, me too. In Pennsylvania. The Susquehanna flooded."

So began a conversation one cold January evening in 1998; my neighbor Lynn Warden and I were trading disaster stories. We didn't finish the conversation that night because we were in the midst of another disaster. He and I were busy working with our families and friends to keep our households functioning during a massive ice storm that had descended upon New York, New England, and eastern Canada. The storm had arrived with little warning, crushing power grids from the Great Lakes to the North Atlantic. It isolated towns, villages, suburbs, neighborhoods, and cities, forced thousands of people into public shelters, and left the remaining several million to struggle in their homes without electricity during the coldest time of the year.

The storm hit particularly hard where I live. And some weeks later, as my family and neighbors began to emerge from the ordeal, I felt a tremendous need to gain some under-standing of those events beyond my own limited perspective. So I began investigating. I interviewed other participants as soon as their lives returned to some semblance of normality. What did they see? How did they cope? I tried to learn more about the power grid: how it was built, how it worked, and why it failed so severely. I also started to examine the way the disaster had been portrayed in a variety of local and national media. I collected newspaper and magazine accounts. I searched the Web for a variety of online reports about the storm. I tracked down transcripts of television news reports and purchased several "ice storm videos" produced by regional television stations and sold as "commemorative edition" keepsakes.

I found the latter items particularly fascinating because they let me reexperience the disaster as I typically experience such events: through television. For hundreds of thousands of us living in the disaster region, television was out for weeks. These videos filled in a lot of the blanks for us. They showed us the storm's impact beyond our neighborhoods or towns. That was interesting, of course, but what I found most compelling was a segment in one video that showed the first moments as a local television station returned to the air under generator power. It was a live nighttime report from a darkened town broadcast just as power was restored to a major substation. The on-location reporter was lit only by car headlights. Then the camera panned across the blackness to security lights blazing for the first time at the drive-up window of a local bank. But something was wrong. The camera turned back toward the substation and focused on flames at the top of a power pole. The reporter was trying to describe what she was seeing when all of a sudden something exploded and everything was black again—save the car headlights, the cascading sparks, and the burning pole.

Many of us up here may have seen such things happen right outside our own homes. But for me, seeing it through the lens of a television camera some months after the storm, the scene conjured up a mix of trauma, excitement, and a strange sense of comfort: it's happening now on the screen and no longer in my front yard.

This book is another screen, another lens trained on those events. It tells stories about two villages separated by time, connected by proximity, and united by the challenges of maintaining a community under duress.

The story of one village presents an insider's view of a natural disaster, describing the destruction of the electric grid in January 1998 and the emergence of a community that filled the resulting void. This story begins with moments in the lives of people in the village of Potsdam, New York—people such as myself, my family, my neighbors, townspeople, local officials, and relief workers—and expands to cover the breadth of the disaster. The book concludes with a timeline of events that traces the disaster from the storm's origins in the Gulf of Mexico to the lethal flooding it caused as it moved slowly up the eastern seaboard to the icy devastation it brought to the Northeast.

The story of the other village begins nearly two hundred years before the ice storm in a place called Louisville Landing, about twenty miles from Potsdam on the border between the United States and Canada. This narrative provides a glimpse of what it took to build the kind of grids that made this nation, the grids that connect us to one another. It is told through the experiences of some of the people who sacrificed the most to build them.

Taken as a whole, these stories become a vehicle by which I examine the relationships between electronic and human connections, between networks and neighborhoods, between grids and villages. We live in a time when one of the foundations of our society, the power grid, appears to be more vulnerable than many of us realized. In New York and California, for example, the demand for power is outstripping the supply. Blackouts and brownouts are on the rise. In the summer of 2000, as power emergencies struck New York City and San Diego, *Time* magazine quoted U.S. Energy Secretary Bill Richardson on the nation's vulnerability: "America is a superpower, but it's got the grid of a Third World nation. If we don't work together and fix the problem, we'll all end up sitting in the dark." But for many of us, it takes the sudden loss of electric power to awaken us to the fragility of the power grid. The stories in this book remind us how vulnerable we are as the demand for power keeps increasing.

These stories also speak to a widespread suspicion that electronic networks in all their forms have, over time, hijacked authentic community life and replaced it with a kind of disaffected placelessness, a networked world of virtual relations driven by personal interest and unchecked consumerism. The book speaks to this issue because its primary story illustrates a time when the global electronic connections went dead for an entire region, thereby providing a glimpse of life suddenly hijacked in another direction: away from the placeless and virtual and toward the local and face to face. And it finds something powerful in that, but troubling, too. Whatever benefits the book finds in locating oneself in a placed community, it also complicates those benefits.

On one level this book is a series of stories about human trauma and recovery. On another it examines how and why we tell such tales. For example, while I based the stories upon a tremendous amount of factual material culled from interviews and eyewitness accounts, I have shaped that material with some common techniques of drama and narrative: I've used violence and suspense, coincidences and cliffhangers. And in Chapter Two, where I've reconstructed a time and place far removed from the reach of any interviewer—the northeastern wilderness at the turn of the nineteenth century, when the social and economic infrastructures of this region were first being built—I've attempted to create a cinematic docudrama of those events. That is, while the other chapters are based solely upon the factual data from my investigation, in Chapter Two I combine historical research with fictional extrapolations. Because we cannot know exactly what happened to some of the long-forgotten settlers of the old wilderness, I have woven together a number of historical accounts with some fictional threads that were inspired by other, complementary historical accounts of the time.

While these threads are, I believe, quite plausible in a historical sense, they also serve to emphasize the cinematic techniques I have used in the rest of the book. In other words, I have laced fiction into one chapter not to set that chapter off from the factual accounts of the rest of the book but rather to *match* the storytelling style of those accounts. This practice highlights the fact that the eyewitness accounts, whether my own or others', are infused with techniques of drama and narrative. Why? Because it is with those techniques that many of us try to make sense of trauma and handle the uncertainties of a difficult time. Ultimately, then, this book finds that regardless of the means of communication—whether electronic or face-to-face—a compulsion to tell stories about one's experience can become an essential way of coping during a crisis. And that, I think, is what has compelled me to collect and trade these tales.

■

I must offer special thanks to Dalton Foster for sharing with me his extensive knowledge of the St. Lawrence Seaway as well as for helping me conduct interviews with some of the last residents of the river's pre-Seaway shoreline. Thanks to all those whom I interviewed about their ice storm experiences or about their lives on the St. Lawrence before the Seaway: Roy Barstow, Al Bradley, Dave and Cindy Centofanti, Carleton Dignean, Frieda Dignean, Judy Funston, John Gamble, Martha Hartle, Marge Howe, Ray Lancto, Stan and Ersel Logan, Terry McKendree, Mark Ryan, Bill Spriggs, Mitch Teich, Lynn and Shirley Warden, Mike and Marge Warden, and Mike Weil.

I also want to thank those who helped me complete this project: Jean Thomson Black, Chris Erikson, and Susan Laity of Yale University Press, Louisville Town Historian Paula Beattie, Pam Cullen, Mark Curran, Brent Faber, Kent Fetter, Laura Gurak, Curt Robinson, Roger Waters, Tom Watson, and the very helpful staff of the Potsdam Public Library.

At the end of another book, *The Wired Neighborhood,* I wrote about driving home from a trip on a cold, clear night in 1995, "when I crested a hill and saw on the farthest northern horizon the faint glow of Montreal." It was "the representation in light of one of the world's great cities . . . a shimmering electric specter" serving for me as both a physical and a psychological marker of where I had been and where I was going. Three years later, while thousands of utility trucks slowly patrolled the night from Lake Ontario to the Atlantic Ocean, the infrastructures that lit Montreal and hundreds of other communities crumbled. Cities, towns, and villages turned dark and myriad stories were born.

The Grid and the Village

one from accidents to disaster

tuesday, january 30, 1996

Buck was a month old when fire licked at the sheetrock by his empty bassinet. I stood at the kitchen counter, ladle in hand, staring out the window at the snow. It seemed to be glowing a golden orange while red embers glided lazily onto the back deck. Kath sat with Buck in the big chair, holding him up on her knee just as our old deckle-edged black and whites showed my mother holding me. I stepped closer to the window. The house was on fire.

I heard a pounding on the front door and it burst open. A woman called out as she ran up the stairs into the light, a stranger darting into the glare of our kitchen hollering at us to get out of our house.

Kath whisked the baby over to the phone and I hurried down the stairs. I called the dogs. The woman was asking me who else was in the house. I told her to take the Subaru across the road to the neighbors' and signaled for the three dogs to jump into the backseat. Onto the good upholstery. They hesitated; something wasn't right. I had to push each one up and in and then I gave the keys and my car and my dogs to a stranger.

A neighbor, Tom, came running down my driveway yelling at me to hook up a hose. Kath ran out of the house with

Buck in a blanket. "I'm taking him to Shirley's," she told me as she hustled him into her car. "Where's your hose?" he yelled again. I could hear a roar coming from the other end of the house, where the new chimney—triple-hulled, stainless steel, high-tech design—was collapsing from the intense heat of a chimney fire. I could see only the tips of the flames from where I stood, but the backyard seemed to be lit ever brighter. The sun had set an hour earlier and the temperature was dropping into the single digits. The garage was chaos. I waded in to find a hose.

I was standing on top of the lawn tractor pushing and pulling at deck chairs when Kath ran back into the garage and then disappeared into the house. I finally found what I was looking for and yanked it out. Tom pulled the hose toward the fire while I tried to hook it up. That's when I got reacquainted with a nice little technological convenience attached to the end of the faucet: a quick-release connector. My end of the hose didn't have the right fitting. I called out to Tom. His end had nothing. I tried to unscrew the connector from the faucet but it was frozen solid. Tom yelled that he needed more hose to get around to the chimney. I dropped my end and ran back into the cluttered darkness of the garage.

I heard cars and a truck pulling up out front just as I found another hose. It had the quick release but the other end was stuck underneath something. A firefighter saw me. "Is there anyone left in the house?" he called. "My wife," I yelled back. Our cat, I thought. Kath had been going in and out with her arms full. Later, I would follow her tracks in the snow to discover a box holding some clothes, the laptop, and the picture albums.

Tom came back with another neighbor, Lynn. I couldn't pull that damn hose out. "The trucks are here," Lynn told me. He said it in a way that meant, Forget the hose. I ran back into the house, where Kath was calling for the cat. The firefighter told us to get out. I could hear for the first time our smoke alarm blaring. I grabbed a coat and walked out. A moment later the firefighter forcibly directed Kath out the door.

As we walked around to the front yard we were confronted with the flashing beacons of fire and rescue trucks. The firefighters, maybe a dozen, worked skillfully, pulling hoses, scaling ladders. They had blocked part of the road and constructed what looked like a big kiddie pool. Two hoses started drenching the roof. Lynn stood next to me with his video camera. One guy up on the roof cranked over a chain-saw engine. I took a deep breath and Lynn put down his camera. "It's a bitch, Steve," he said.

We continued to watch as they broke through the walls and cut through the roof, water cannonading into every suspicious space. The chimney lay blackened and twisted in the backyard, part of it crushed by the wood-burning stove that had been lifted and tossed out through a big hole in the wall. Within a half hour most of the event was over. One of the firefighters had to be treated for smoke inhalation.

When the chief let us back in, he apologized for all of the tramping over soaked rugs. A couple of the firefighters offered to nail a big tarp over the roof to keep the snow out if we could supply hammers and nails. We did. The chief stood in the kitchen and told us that based on his inspection he had decided not to call the power company to kill power because the service drop came in at the opposite end of the house and hadn't been damaged. "That'll let you keep some heat up in here," he said. "Your pipes won't freeze and then maybe you can get someone to button up the other end soon." We thanked him and everyone else. The cat scooted out of a downstairs closet. Lynn told us to come over for the night whenever we were ready.

I found the Subaru parked across the road with the dogs inside, curled tightly against the bitter cold. We took them to Lynn and Shirley's where each of us hugged Buck tight in the warmth of their kitchen. Later, I went back over to the dank, stinking cave of a house to search for insurance papers, move some furniture, and begin what would later seem like weeks of mopping up water.

The next morning we made the local radio news. Somehow the report included the fact that we had house insurance. Since when is that public information? I wondered. That day's edition of the local paper had a front-page picture of a dark, yawning hole into our bedroom with a caption that also mentioned the insurance. If I hadn't felt like a victim before, I did then, and I didn't like it one damn bit. I reacted as if it wasn't the fire but the local media that had broken through that wall and put our bedroom on display. But what else were the local reporters supposed to do? Around here house fires are news, and quite often those stories say something like, the so-and-so family had no insurance and donations can be made to the XYZ agency to help them recover from the accident. When I hear this about others, I think: community members helping each other. Great. After my brush with the experience, I was thinking that there was something incompatible between news coverage and personal privacy.

The caption also mentioned that we had been alerted to the fire by a neighbor. To this day I have no idea who she was.

A couple of weeks later another neighbor's chimney caught fire, and even though that house suffered no damage, suddenly we were all talking about scrapping the woodstoves. And one by one each house on our little stretch of country road switched over to an alternative heat source: at Cindy and Dave's across the way, at our house, and eventually two doors down at Lynn and Shirley's. With that we all became completely dependent on one key element, electricity. One way or another it would provide light and heat and draw water from our wells. I never gave it a thought.

tuesday, august 27, 1996

Shirley Warden always seems so happy to see you. Whether she's walking her dogs on the road or working in the yard, she has a big smile and waves enthusiastically to her neighbors. Even when she's driving by the horn blares: you jump, shocked by the blast, there's a flash of waving hand and there goes Shirley barreling down the road.

But not on this night. As I pushed the stroller past the Wardens' driveway on a mild summer evening seven months after our fire, I heard a screen door open and watched Shirley hurry to her car. A curt "Hi, Steve," and nothing else. No stop for chat, no smile for the baby, just a car-door slam and off she went. That seemed odd.

A while later I got the word: Lynn had been in an accident. It would be days before I learned the details but right away it was clear that it was something terrible. That night he was being transported by ambulance to the Fletcher Allen medical center in Burlington, Vermont, three hours to the east. His doctor in Potsdam wanted to have him airlifted to the center but no aircraft was available. It was a difficult ride; he had lost a lot of blood.

Lynn is a stocky guy; fiftysomething, strong, hardworking. He's the head of security for a regional drugstore chain and he's worked in law enforcement and security all his adult life. That night he had been driving his company car back home after visiting stores downstate when he came upon a bridge under construction. As Lynn guided the car toward a one-lane detour to the right of the bridge, suddenly the butt end of a temporary guardrail caught the front of the car just below the driver's-side headlight and just above the front tire, exploding through the floorboard, knifing through his leg, and slamming him into the backseat.

Sitting apparently unharmed in the front was the car phone, his only link to anyone else on this sparsely traveled road. But he couldn't reach it and he couldn't move. Fifteen miles from nowhere on a back road with no one else around, he had a problem, as he put it later. Somehow he had the wherewithal to pull off his tie, slide it around his leg, and tighten it. The tourniquet kept him from bleeding to death. It took the Jaws of Life to get him out of the car.

But the leg was gone and it would be weeks before we'd see him again. And yet by the following January, with the help of his family, friends, coworkers, and his own drive to overcome the obstacles before him, Lynn returned to work full time. That involved going back out on the road and fulfilling all the duties he'd had before the accident. During the next year he would still go to hunting camp at his family's cabin downstate and I'd still see him out cutting the grass, plowing snow, building decks, and repairing docks. The only difference was that, in addition to his prosthetic leg and all of the daunting challenges associated with it, he was aided by more communication devices: a fax machine and e-mail at home and a cell phone for his pocket. If he needed to contact anyone, anywhere, anytime, the communications grid was always there.

monday, january 5, to wednesday, january 7, 1998

Two years before Lynn's ordeal began, a good friend of his had been called out to the scene of another violent accident. State Trooper Leo Grant was one of many local emergency-response personnel summoned to a nearby stretch of road, where they found a crushed Chevy Blazer, an overturned dumptruck, and three fatalities. The Blazer had been traveling west on Route 11, a two-lane highway that extends across northern New York from Lake Champlain in the east to Lake Ontario in the west. A few miles out of Potsdam an approaching dumptruck loaded with asphalt blew a tire and began to cross the center line into oncoming traffic. It sideswiped one car and slammed head-on into the Blazer. The driver of the Blazer—the only one wearing a seatbelt—her sister, and her mother-in-law were all killed instantly.

The accident became the cause of litigation against the trucking firm, and eventually against both the asphalt company that had loaded the truck and St. Lawrence County, which had contracted for the services of both companies. One trial resulted in a conviction of the trucking firm but that verdict was overturned on appeal. A second case, a civil suit against the asphalt company and the county, went to trial in the first full week of the new year, 1998.

On Monday, January 5, prospective jurors traveled to the St. Lawrence County Courthouse through some nasty weather. What was supposed to be the first day back to school after New Year's turned out to be another holiday for the kids, and a day of treacherous driving for everyone who had to travel across this sparsely populated expanse of borderlands known to residents as "the north country." A major storm laden with moisture had been moving slowly up the East Coast. It brought floods to the south and mid-Atlantic but up north a cold front held stubbornly to the ground. As the warmer storm spread northward it began to slide above the cold front, dropping rain down into twenty-degree temperatures. Everything started icing up.

Judy Funston was one of those who had to negotiate the roads to the courthouse that morning, having been called to join the pool of potential jurors. Originally from Michigan, Judy had been on the faculty of SUNY Potsdam for the past eight years and lived with her plants and animals—a house rabbit, two cats, and an aquarium—a few miles north of the village. Living alone, she valued both her privacy and the regularity of a set schedule, a daily routine that was interrupted as she sat in the courtroom listening to lawyers outline the tragic circumstances of the violent accident.

On Tuesday, Judy was dismissed from the jury pool, and she left the courthouse shaken by the horror and caprice of what had happened out on Route 11 three years earlier. Although she couldn't have known it then, for her those two days in court were merely the start of a time both traumatic and exhilarating. As she drove home that afternoon, taking the same route the victims had taken the day they were killed, she couldn't know that in a month a similarly chilling and random misfortune would visit her family. She couldn't know that in her hometown of Ypsilanti the sister she was closest to would be broadsided in her car by a pickup truck running a red light, throwing her across the front seat into the passenger door while crushing the roof onto the spot where her head would have been had she been wearing a seatbelt. Her sister would need extensive surgery, having suffered broken ribs, a fractured pelvis, and a lacerated spleen.

Nor could Judy have known that within days of leaving the courtroom she would become engaged in events that not only would shatter the daily routine that she prized but would transform her relationships with people around her in Potsdam as well as with her family back in Michigan. She could not have predicted that she would be drawn into work through which she would find common purpose with a whole range of people in the community, people such as Lynn Warden and Leo Grant; such as Al Bradley, a technician for Niagara

Mohawk Power Corporation; such as Martha Hartle, a full-time college administrator and part-time emergency medical technician; such as Mitch Teich, a North Country Public Radio reporter; and many, many others. She could not have known that she would soon play a small role in maintaining the social grid, a network of strangers with whom she had nothing in common but location and circumstance. It would be difficult work—rewarding, at times harrowing, and most significantly it would be work that she hadn't known she was capable of doing.

As Judy traveled back to Potsdam that Tuesday in still more icy rain, Lynn Warden was 150 miles away in Syracuse listening to the weather forecasts and thinking about driving home to a house that no longer had a wood-burning stove. I sat in my office in the village thinking about another grid, the media grid, the web of electronic connectivity that shapes our lives in ever more powerful ways. This was the topic of a new course about the social impacts of computers that I was scheduled to begin teaching the following week. Yes, I was aware of the storm, but only because it was impinging upon this work. On Monday our daycare provider, Marge Howe, had decided that travel was too chancy to come to work, giving me another vacation day at home with my son. With schools closed again on Tuesday, Marge called to tell me that she was coming in but would probably need to leave early given the road conditions. Kath had been able to get to the Alcoa plant twenty-five miles to the north where she worked as an engineer, so it was up to me to cut my work short. No problem, I told her. I just needed a few hours to organize the syllabus.

As I described it, the course would focus on "media literacy for a networked world."[1] Students would learn how the Internet and the Web have evolved into a new kind of commercial mass media. They would explore the relationships between these new media and the handful of giant media corporations that encompass vast complexes of television, radio, movies, book publishing, telecom, computers, software, and the like. In addition, I wanted students to go beyond mindless viewership and begin to think about the relationships between electronic media and consumer behavior. I wanted them to recognize how images of social and sexual power—often exerted violently—are used to deliver customers to advertising and how unrelentingly advertising wends its way into all public spaces, and most private ones. Finally, to make the crucial connection between computers and advertising, I wanted them to understand how advertisers seek to reach very specific markets by taking advantage of the capabilities of a whole range of computer-based targeting technologies. We may be connected to a vast media grid, but within that complex we can be identified as very specific consumers in ever more sophisticated ways.

This view of the media, promoted by a variety of media literacy activists, had become my view too. It justified my job, which I have increasingly seen as the teaching of media literacy. But as I left work and drove home on slickening roads that afternoon, I couldn't help feeling that this whole line of reasoning had become too pat for me. My media literacy lectures seemed more and more like a product I was selling, replete with videos, Websites, student research projects, and term papers. Something was amiss but I didn't quite know what.

Another thing I didn't know as I outlined this course about culturemaking electronic grids was that my local grids—power, cable T.V., Internet, and telephone services—were just beginning to become stressed. In the north country, as in any large rural area, it takes a lot of wire and materials to connect a small number of customers. The five counties that spread across the top of New York cover an area the size of

Massachusetts but with just a fraction of its population. Potsdam is one of the population centers of the region, yet even when both colleges, SUNY Potsdam and Clarkson, are in session, the number of residents maxes out at only around ten thousand.

Of course it wasn't just northern New York under duress on this day. Ice was building across eastern Ontario and southern Quebec, including parts of the city of Ottawa and most of the Montreal metropolitan region; it was forming in isolated patches of Vermont and New Hampshire and spreading across a large swath of Maine and into the Canadian Maritimes. The job of maintaining the grids crisscrossing the great northeastern forests, challenging in normal times, was getting even more difficult.

While I unwittingly consumed the fruits of such infrastructures in my well-lit, well-connected, and comfortably heated office, those whose job it was to maintain the grids were watching the wires. The regional manager for Time Warner Cable—yes, media giants reach up here, too—had noticed as early as Sunday night that ice was collecting on wires. By Tuesday morning maybe a hundred customers were reporting outages, and by later that day the manager called downstate for some extra line crews just in case.

Likewise, managers and technicians for Niagara Mohawk (NiMo), the large utility serving northern and western New York, were also concerned. Al Bradley couldn't help but notice some buildup Tuesday morning on his way to work. He anticipated trouble in the grid, but when he stopped in first thing at the NiMo service center in Potsdam, he was surprised to see that very few line trucks had been called out to investigate power outages. The line crews are the ones who are dispatched in any weather at any time to repair and reenergize damaged distribution lines—the lines that run to homes and businesses.

Maybe things aren't so bad after all, he thought as he drove out of town to continue his normal day-to-day work as a relay and control technician for the other side of the system, the high-power transmission grid.

Al had been working at a large substation near the town of Gouverneur, thirty-five miles southwest of Potsdam. All the way there the lines and trees were icy, but by early afternoon when he walked out of the substation much of it appeared to have thawed. The storm is turning over to rain, he thought. We're home free.

He left Gouverneur at 2 P.M. and headed back to Potsdam. When he got about ten miles out, right around a little town named DeKalb, he crossed a line from water into ice. This is unreal, he thought. Within maybe a quarter mile conditions went from no ice to ice everywhere. As he got closer to Canton it got worse and worse. By the time he made it back to Potsdam he said to himself, We're in trouble. He left work at three, ran some errands, got home about quarter to four and the phone rang as he was taking off his boots. It was his supervisor asking him to come back to work. He was told extra crews from downstate had been called and would be arriving soon. He needed to report back, not to his department but to the line department instead. He was heading out into the storm.

Forty miles to the east, outside the town of Malone, outages were cropping up in isolated areas. Al was told that at any moment five line crews from Watertown were going to show up and he was to take them to Malone, where he would report to the line supervisor. Although Al had returned with just the clothes on his back, figuring he'd be working locally, he and the crews headed out of town on the main highway east, State Route 11B. Leading the convoy in a NiMo van, Al brought them to the Malone office by early evening.

There he was told to take the crews to a remote substation near the Akwesasne Mohawk Reservation just south of the Canadian border and have them start to patrol every circuit coming out of that sub. Each circuit is a loop bringing power to customers and all of them had gone dead. It was up to Al to decide how to use the crews. He could split them up and send them in five different directions or keep them together to put all resources in the worst areas. Al was told to call back for a tree crew if they ran into anything that demanded one. Tree crews are equipped to cut down large trees and limbs while line crews are equipped only with standard chain saws and can handle only smaller trees. The workers' primary task was to find places where tree limbs had knocked down wires and do whatever they could to get those wires back up quickly. And that's what they did through the night. When they returned to the Malone office around daybreak, Al thought the worst of it might be over, but he was told to report back in six hours. He and the crews were to stay in a local motel.

Around the time Al checked in, forty miles away I was waking up on autopilot, assuming life would be returning to normal. As usual, Kath had already left for work and I expected Marge to arrive in an hour, freeing me to go to the office and continue preparing for the upcoming semester. But when I turned on North Country Public Radio and glanced out the window, I discovered that the schools were closed again and the trees in my backyard were still glistening. Only now I was hearing something new. The weather forecasters were talking about the potential of heavy icing starting late in the day. Marge wouldn't be arriving.

Like any empirical research, determining what the weather will be up here requires multiple sources of data and a dose of interpretation. While the region may be linked to vast communication grids, holes in our connectivity are still apparent. There are no television stations located in St. Lawrence County, the largest county in the state and one of the largest east of the Mississippi River. Nor are there any in neighboring Franklin County to the east. National Weather Service reports for the area are provided by North Country Public Radio and by WPDM, the one Potsdam F.M. station, but if you want some visual data, you need to triangulate among T.V. stations in Ottawa; Burlington, Vermont; and Watertown, New York, mix and match Celsius and Fahrenheit readings, then consult the unrelenting Weather Channel and its colorful local forecast maps. If you have Web access at home—thanks to a balky modem I didn't at the time—there are what appear to be targeted predictions for the north country. But I have been suspicious of all claims of accuracy ever since my brother bought me one of those dedicated weather radios you can get from outdoors catalogs. Just turn it on anywhere in the country—anywhere—and you instantly get continual local weather reports from the National Weather Service. Anywhere but here, that is. It didn't work then and still doesn't. Apparently there's a hole in the coverage up here on the fringes.

Nonetheless, I hit the remote in search of more data, and on came cable T.V. But while I could still weather surf, more and more people in the region were unable to do so. Time Warner Cable was losing ground. By midmorning there were roughly a thousand customers without cable, a tenfold increase in twenty-four hours despite stepped-up service efforts. The number of outages wasn't alarming but the trend was. In particular, the "house drops"—the cable connections from the streets to houses—were beginning to fall at a rate that outpaced repairs.

Lynn Warden had also been watching the Weather Channel before leaving for work from his motel room in warm and foggy Syracuse. Back home, Shirley, who works as a nurse at St.

Lawrence University in nearby Canton, had some concerns. Not only was Lynn on the road but her son and daughter-in-law, Mike and Marge, who live a mile across the river from our houses, were expecting the birth of their second child at any time. So by noon Shirley called Lynn just in case he hadn't heard the forecasts. But of course he had and he'd already made a decision that he'd been mulling over ever since the demise of the wood-burning stoves. That day, before leaving the city, he would buy a portable, gas-powered generator. If there was ever a time, he thought, it's now.

Of course, numerous other warning calls went out across the north country that morning. One went to the president of Clarkson University from his executive assistant, Martha Hartle. The president had been working in Albany, the state capital, four hours to the south, and Martha urged him to leave for home earlier than planned. By then the decision had been made to close the university at noon. Shortly thereafter, with the president's office deserted by all save Martha, the power failed. But because there was enough outside light in her office, she decided to stay and finish up the day's work. As she sat near one of the large wood-framed windows that grace the hundred-year-old building, Martha suddenly heard a loud cracking outside. She jumped and ran into an inner office as a tree split, missing the window but taking down an electrical wire. When she slowly returned to see what had happened, she saw sparks among the branches. Out there somewhere was power, and it was arcing.

For Martha the danger of the storm was very real, but many others knew nothing about the forecasts and went about their business as normally as they could given the messy state of the roads. Kath found herself in marathon meetings at work, where she and two other engineers had scheduled a dozen interviews with job candidates. The interviews took place in an office that had no view of the outside, no telephone, and no radio. They would get the interviews done that day no matter how long it took them. Back in Potsdam Judy Funston also made it to her office for the first time that week and tried to catch up on e-mail, voice mail, snail mail, and the like. Later, at home, she decided to clean her house, and spent the next several hours dusting, watering plants, cleaning the rabbit's cage, and washing the floors before heading off to buy groceries. It was in the store that she first heard something about a new storm.

In the afternoon, with my son napping and my teaching materials spread across the dining room table, I tried to focus on what wasn't right about the media course. I found it difficult to concentrate. I had just tried to reach Kath at work but I couldn't locate her, so I sat back down and scanned the list of videos I had collected for the course. If I had wanted to, I could have wallpapered the semester with videos, from a series on the history of computers, to documentaries about media powerbrokers like Rupert Murdoch, to critical analyses of the power of advertising, to explorations of the ways digital media invade our privacy. One of those tapes contained a speech about media propaganda by Mark Crispin Miller, an engaging, influential media critic, writer, and teacher whose work I admire greatly. As videos go, it's pretty dull—it's a C-SPAN recording of Miller speaking at New York University—but the argument he made I found both powerful and troubling. In particular, I was thinking about one key moment near the end of the speech when someone in the audience asked a question that seemed to startle Miller. It had startled me too the first time I had heard it, and perhaps this was the source of what had been bothering me about my course plan.

In his talk Miller pointed out that what many people think of as propaganda is based on a very narrow definition that arose through half a century of cold war between western democracies and their communist counterparts. Over that time the term *propaganda* became equated with classic communist rhetoric; those leaden harangues about the joys of collectivism and the evils of capitalism. Contrary to this view, argued Miller, propaganda at its best is the slick, snappy product that comes from today's corporate media giants; that is, the most effective propaganda is that which is emotional and engaging but only surreptitiously persuasive. The purpose of corporate propaganda is, of course, the furthering of the corporate interests. One corporate interest is limiting the power and scope of the public sector.

What was wrong here started to become clearer to me during the Q&A session near the end of the Miller speech, when a member of the audience pointed out that the speech was part of a series of talks sponsored by New York University, a major benefactor of which is former CBS mogul Lawrence Tisch.

I'm a big fan of your writing and I appreciate you coming tonight. I'm a little bit cynical about the us-and-them split in that it seems a lot messier than "They're committing propaganda and we're telling the truth." Several people have alluded to it [earlier in the Q&A], but in my vague and very limited knowledge of the way this works—and a lot of this is actually inspired by your writing—there is a connection between Larry Tisch and CBS and this very university and the fact that you're speaking here tonight. There are a good percentage of my colleagues—myself and several other people—that are employed by these four monoliths [the major corporate media giants], which are paying for our education to come learn what terrible propagandists they are. [Scattered laughter in the audience.] So my question is, couldn't an argument be made just as easily that media critics like you are just the best form of entertainment for intellectuals like us? [Big laughter.]

In other words, isn't this media literacy stuff just another form of propaganda; isn't propaganda inseparable from advocacy and aren't all advocates operating in the same entertainment marketplace that turns all public discourse into mere selling of positions? Wasn't I just attempting to manipulate my students into agreeing with me that what I do for a living, teaching media literacy, is something they need? Isn't this just like selling beer, cars, deodorant, political candidates, the evening news, or any other product?

Miller's response to the audience member's comment was that most people don't know much about the power and deceptions of corporate media and are enlightened by these arguments. If true, that means there are markets yet to reach with the media literacy sales pitch. As I write this two years later, Hollywood has crafted some new products for those of us interested in critiques of corporate media. Isn't the success of corporate Hollywood in satirizing and revealing the agendas of big media in big-budget, big–box office movies like *The Truman Show* and *The Insider* the ultimate illustration of the propaganda/entertainment box from which we can't escape? Big media has gripping stories to tell about its stranglehold on our consciousness. And the soundtrack CDs are really good too! (And isn't a book like the one you are reading using standard corporate media techniques in order to compete in its own small marketplace?)

I sat there jotting notes about some of this when (in a manner not unlike the ringing of a telephone used to move

characters on and off camera) I heard a cry from my son's bedroom and I knew work was over for the day. Just as well, I
thought; I should probably tend to things around the house in
case the storm actually does get worse.

Many people were only mildly concerned about the predicted icing. At North Country Public Radio, reporter Mitch
Teich knew the forecast quite well but didn't anticipate anything more than the normal inconveniences of a winter
storm—the usual long list of cancellations to be announced on
air the next morning. Likewise, Potsdam Village Police Chief
Terry McKendree was a bit skeptical about the potential impact of the impending weather. He had seen threatening
storms come and go numerous times before with little or no
trouble. When Hurricane Hugo took an inland route from the
Carolinas and shot up through eastern Ontario in 1989, there
were some branches down here and there, but it caused very
little damage overall. In 1993 the "Storm of the Century," the
great snowstorm that lumbered up the eastern seaboard,
killing more than two hundred people and shutting down city
after city, pounded the north country, but without dire results.

Nonetheless, by early evening Chief McKendree had
had some conversations with the village supervisor, Mike
Weil, about contingency plans. Mike had been contacting
the key services that might be needed if there were indeed
an emergency. He and the Potsdam town supervisor (in
government-happy New York there are both town and village
administrators) had made up a list of personnel from the
schools, agencies, fire department, road crew, hospital, and the
like, split it up, and started calling to discuss plans. They decided to establish a site for an emergency shelter and they
called people at the SUNY Potsdam physical plant to see if
Maxcy Hall, the large gymnasium and field house, could serve.
In general, they began the process of energizing the emer-

gency public service grid, a quasi–network of individuals within the village, town, and county. Although she didn't know it at the time, Martha Hartle's name would be added to Mike Weil's list.

As official Potsdam was beginning to form its emergency plans, Lynn's son Mike and Dave Centofanti, our neighbor from across the road, were carrying the new generator down to Lynn and Shirley's basement. Lynn had gotten home around 5 P.M. and witnessed the same change Al Bradley had seen the day before. About fifty miles from home, he had entered a world encapsulated within ice, growing thicker and thicker the closer he got to Potsdam.

As Mike and Dave, fellow football coaches in the Potsdam school district, eased the box across the lawn, Mike was amazed that his six–foot–two, 240-pound frame could not break through the milky layer of ice that had built up across the yard. Lynn noticed that too, well aware that the worst of the predicted big storm hadn't yet arrived.

Like Lynn, Dave and his wife, Cindy, had considered buying a generator, but decided against it. It seemed like a big expense for something they would use rarely, if ever. Even so, Dave had gone out earlier to buy some fuel for his camp stove but had discovered that it was already sold out everywhere. He had also noticed that one of the limbs of a willow in his front yard had begun to hang across his electric service drop, so he had called NiMo to send out a tree crew to cut it.

Around 7 P.M. Kath's group had to decide whether or not to continue after the final interviewee told them about the impending storm. After some discussion the group agreed to stay on for a short while so they could compare notes and discuss candidates. When they finally left the building they were all stunned to see the amount of ice that had built up on their cars. And on the horizon they saw flashes—short, bright explosions of some kind. Kath switched on the four-wheel drive and headed home very slowly. By the time she arrived I had distributed some candles and flashlights upstairs and down and filled the bathtub with water. A couple of miles away Judy Funston had drawn buckets of water and collected her candles and matches. Later she would go to bed nervous about what might happen during the night. Around nine, Lynn glanced out the window and saw what looked like searchlights moving down the road. He realized it was a NiMo crew cutting trees. A few moments later the power went out. There he sat in the dark, with his new generator still in the box.

The spreading darkness started to worry Al Bradley as he and the linemen, aided by a big tree crew, worked through the night. They were spending a lot of time repairing circuits only to see them crash again a few hours later. Although frustrating, this wasn't without precedent in past icing situations. Typically, a crew might decide against cutting large trees because people don't like to have their trees cut. Instead the crew will just put the circuit back up knowing that more branches could come down and take it out again. Or sometimes they repair the circuit while leaving branches hanging below the wires, only to have those branches pop up during a thaw a day later, possibly bringing down the circuit one more time. Given the choice between unhappy customers without power and unhappy customers without trees, the crews tend to feel a damned-if-you-do-damned-if-you-don't tension during these events.

But Al began to realize that this storm was presenting an even worse problem. Not only were the trees taking out lines, but the weight of the ice on the wires was beginning to reach a critical mass. Entire poles were snapping under it. Poles out in fields with nothing around them were snapping one after another.

Late Wednesday night he was told to head out to one of

the rural areas where major damage had been reported. He was to take some tree crews to clean up the area and then call the line crews to restore the lines. The roads were black, the rain heavy, and the truck headlights cut a path, refracting and twinkling amid gleaming branches. Al held slips of paper with messages indicating where there might be large trees down on the lines. Around midnight, while they were looking for one of these spots, they stopped in the darkness. Al wasn't sure just where they were and he was training a flashlight beam up and down a pole looking for a number to get his bearings, when suddenly the sky toward the west lit up. Everyone in the trucks yelled. Then it happened again. Al turned his flashlight to his circuit maps to try to figure out if the explosion might have happened on a high-powered transmission line, or if it was just another distribution line. He couldn't be sure, so he got back on the radio and called the line supervisor in Malone and said, "Hey, there's something really arcing off in the west." The supervisor replied that they had just lost circuits out that way. Then he said, "Forget what I sent you on. Go find out what that is."

So they took off patrolling among the lonely blacktops that crisscross the flatlands near the northern border of the Adirondack Park. They passed a couple of small side roads and then came upon a lone volunteer fireman waving a flashlight next to his car. The blue light on the roof pulsed and Al couldn't help but notice that he had a wide-eyed, stunned look. "Something big is happening up there," he told Al, pointing up into the darkness.

The big trucks turned slowly and began lumbering up the road, where they eventually came upon a large tree perched just so, about to tear down a line. Al got out while the tree cutters started riding the bucket up. As Al stood in the road, trees crashed in the woods in back of him, across the road, all around, continually popping and cracking in every direction. Here we are, he thought, our nerves are raw and we're taking down this ice-coated tree and we're hearing the woods crashing and we're thinking that these limbs can come down on our heads and these hardhats aren't going to stop them. One of them will drive a man right into the ground. The men in the buckets were right there underneath the falling canopy. They'd cut one limb and five or six more would come down with it. It's a dangerous place to be, Al thought. You can't run. It's slippery underfoot. It's just a bad position to be in.

origins of a grid, part 1

Until recently, I hadn't known much about how electric power got to my house or to anyone else's. Like most people, I never thought about the power grid until the lights went out (or thought about the cable connections until the set went snowy, or the phone lines until I no longer had a dial tone). And even then I'd usually respond with a "Hey, get my service back." But a couple of years ago I found myself in a discussion about power generation that finally started to open my eyes to its significance to the work I do. I had been researching the relationships between network communications and local communities when I had the opportunity to visit the city of Odense, Denmark, to participate in an academic conference. While there, I was struck by how nicely blended the city's residential and commercial sectors were. The city had the look and feel of a small town while still encompassing a full range of urban commerce. It looked to me as though one could live in a pleasant, affordable neighborhood and still be able to walk or bike easily to all services, shopping, and entertainment.

By chance one of my hosts and I began talking about how his home in the city was heated. A centralized power plant generated heat that was distributed to homes and businesses throughout the city. "You mean you don't have a furnace in your house?" I asked. "No," he said, and went on to explain how the power plant and the city evolved. As he spoke, it became clear that power generation played a significant role in maintaining not only the city's physical infrastructure, its streets and buildings, but its social infrastructures as well. Power generation and community were deeply entwined.

So I started to do a little reading in the area, and when it came time to choose books for one of the media courses I teach I briefly considered requiring David Nye's *Electrifying America,* a fascinating, lucid history and analysis of the evolution of electric power from the late nineteenth century through the first half of the twentieth.

My thinking was that while my students are continually told that they live in revolutionary times, Nye's book would offer a glimpse of a period of unprecedented change, a time that went from candles and oil lamps, outhouses, and hand-cranked wells to electric light, indoor plumbing, telephone, and radio within the span of an adult lifetime. It could be good for students to understand that this revolution was driven not only by what we might call "useful" purposes—electricity needed to run a more productive manufacturing process, for example— but also by the desire to energize spectacular, marginally functional commercial and social phenomena: searchlights playing to and fro across a department store, arc lights illuminating the imposing walls of a mansion, the "great white ways" drawing people to center cities. Furthermore, the expanding market for electric power enabled individuals and communities to see beyond local, parochial barriers. Not only did the spread of electric grids connect individuals to a network, they connected communities to national networks, national institutions, and a national culture "of which the movies, amusement parks, and radio stations were only the most obvious parts."[1] At the same time, this commercial force delivered services to a vast demographic. Electrification was "the most democratically dispersed modern utility," said Nye. Even at the height of the Great Depression, in 1934, urban areas were almost universally wired.[2]

While the expanding patchwork of grids fueled the development of cities, these grids eventually broke the city's hold as the central source of essential services. The spread of electrification enabled a retreat from the city; it enabled homes to exist outside of the urban service center. Home refrigerators, for example, severed the connection to the ice deliveries available in the urban centers as well as the need to live within walking distance of grocery stores. Unlike in Denmark, where Nye has lived and which he discussed near the end of the book, "Americans used the flexibility of electrical power to atomize society rather than to integrate it. Electricity permitted them to intensify individualism as they rejected centralized communal services in favor of personal control over less efficient but autonomous appliances."[3] Such choices went hand-in-hand with the rise of large commercial power companies and the waning of local municipal utilities.

The ways Americans chose to develop their power grids shaped the kind of lives they could lead. And, of course, electric power has become a foundation upon which we live. In an age characterized by mistrust in institutions and sources of authority, few question the necessity of electric power. Yes, there are industries that generate and sell other energy sources and yes, there are those who choose to live off the electric grid and yes, there are movements to deregulate the power industry and promote local, even personal alternatives, but for most people there is no alternative to living with electric power in one form or another. For the majority, electric power is beyond the range of debate.

Which is probably why most of us focus on this fundamental infrastructure only when it is interrupted. Even reading Nye's history had its limitations for me. While it helped to make me more mindful of power grids in general, it wasn't until I was compelled to trace parts of my regional grid back in time—to see it through both the work of historians and the accounts of local eyewitnesses—that I began to get a better understanding of what it took to build these grids. The narrative that follows illustrates this understanding.

Two hundred years ago, a long-forgotten band of adventurers started building an infrastructure across a vast wilderness. It began in a little-known stretch of land some twenty miles north of my home. But the process had been set forth by decree in New York City and was motivated by this nation's tenuous hold on sovereignty in the years just after the Revolutionary War. These endeavors, as I have reconstructed them here and in Chapter Four, culminated in the completion of an immense component of the region's modern power grid: the St. Lawrence Seaway, constructed a century and a half later during the two decades of can-do optimism that followed the Second World War.

Forty years after that, as the ice storm descended upon the region's communications and power infrastructures, millions were cut off from those grids and left cold and isolated—two conditions of life that have a long heritage up here.

winter 1816

Louis Gerteau knew where there was money, a lot of money, and he planned to take it. The cash lay unprotected, he had heard, in a house near a tiny village named Louisville on the edge of the last wilderness left in the northeastern states. It was the house where his brother-in-law, Jean Baptiste Macue, lived. Macue worked for a lumberman named Michael Scarborough and took a room in Scarborough's house, where the lumberman's wife, son, and infant daughter lived. It was late February and Scarborough was traveling on business. He had left Macue in charge until his return.

On the night of February 21, Louis Gerteau huddled in secret inside the Scarborough barn. Shortly before dawn, carrying a scythe he had found in the barn, he moved on the house. Discovering the door unlocked, he stepped inside and determined that everyone was asleep. By the door he spied an ax, which he silently traded for the scythe.

He stepped cautiously through the room where Macue lay and continued on to the bedroom of Mrs. Scarborough and her children. There, in a corner drawer, he found the cash. At this moment he might have escaped without harm but Scarborough began to stir. Gerteau turned and wielded the ax, slamming it down on the woman's neck, nearly severing her head. He immediately turned back toward the children, killing the infant with a quick snap of the instrument and leaving the other unconscious and bleeding. In seconds he burst in on his brother-in-law and dispatched him with several sure blows to the head. Having silenced his victims, he stopped in the kitchen for a moment and ate a few cakes and sweetmeats before departing the house as quietly as he had entered it. He tightly fastened the door and fled with the twenty-two dollars that had motivated the crime.

Within the hour a neighbor came by to check on the family and thought it odd that the door had been fastened from the outside. Looking in a window, the neighbor could see part of the horror. After breaking open the door and seeing the extent of the massacre, he ran outside and discovered tracks in the snow heading off to the east. Spreading an alarm, the neighbor rounded up a searching party and set out to track the killer.

Gerteau had not been traveling very fast. At one point he stopped in the woods and tried unsuccessfully to clean the blood off his clothes. He was overtaken by his pursuers a couple of miles outside of St. Regis, the village of the Kanien'keha:ka (the Mohawks) and forcibly returned to the Scarborough house, where he admitted his crime and produced the stolen money.

At that moment his captors had a decision to make. They could dispense a swift and total retribution by tying him to a tree and shooting him. They could hang him. They could enact a reciprocal revenge by turning the bloodied ax on this monster. For a crime so ghastly, these men could have argued that any fatal punishment would be justified. They lived on the edge of a frontier. The northern forests stretched for hundreds of miles in every direction, bisected by the great ice-choked river. The killer's remains might wash ashore miles below and months later.

If the captors carried out their own sentence, who would ever know?

ten years earlier, january 6, 1806

Strands of red hair flickered across her pale cheek as she stood on the porch watching the ghostly shape of a silent animal bounding through the new snow. She knew it was just the dog following wisps of scent floating across the unbroken white surface before her. Dawn had broken and she'd be needing a scarf soon. A wind was coming up. Behind her, distracted with his gear, Abner Powell didn't seem to hear her question. Again she asked, "Are you taking Mr. Bear with you, Father?" But he was already walking away along the length of the porch and down into the snow, knapsack over one shoulder, powder horn at his belt, and muzzle-loader in hand. She knew where he was headed: across the field to the cut and then to the river. Suddenly he stopped and looked about, as if realizing that Amanda had indeed been speaking to him. Had she wanted something? he called back.

The young girl ran toward her father and, despite his warnings to stay out of the snow, joined him in the field, hugging him around the waist. How soon would he return? she wanted to know. Before dark? She demanded that he come home before dark. Mr. Bear circled the two of them and then suddenly disappeared inside the barn, setting off the cow, who was easily agitated by the dog. Smiling, Powell shouldered his musket and bent over to pick her up, to embrace and reassure her. But Amanda's eyes would have none of it. Describing the girl a half century later, Franklin Hough, in the first comprehensive history of this region, would write that at that moment she felt "an instinctive foreboding of evil."[4] She hugged him hard around the neck and kissed his cheek. The swirling winds scattered her hair about his face.

Where Powell and his daughter stood was a difficult place. There were dangers even for those leading the most mundane of lives. Many white men and women feared the native Haudenosaunee, the Iroquois, who were being systematically displaced from these aboriginal territories. Some feared the British army and its surrogates in Upper and Lower Canada, who still haunted the nearby boundary waters. Many feared a God who would show sinners and nonbelievers His wrath by bringing severe winter weather and starvation down upon those whose faith was not strong enough. Some feared the wolves who always seemed to circle just out of sight. Yet despite these fears, or because of them, these people persisted in cutting trees and tilling the soil; their surveyors chopped their sight lines, marking the white man's divisions of the wilderness, their farmers cleared fields and planted domesticated crops, their lumbermen cut timber and floated it down the rivers.

This was land that only twenty years before was largely unknown to the white man. A 1785 map labeled it "Irocoisia," another referred to it as the deer hunting grounds of the Iroquois, and another called it "Coughsagrage," the Haudenosaunee's beaver hunting lands. To the white man it was a vast terra incognita bound on the north by the St. Lawrence River, on the east and west by the large lakes, Champlain and Ontario, and on the south by the Mohawk River valley, where the last outpost of civilization, Fort Stanwix, was located. Yet despite the legacy of natives' claims to the region, the state of New York initiated its exploration and settlement by layering the image of order atop its indeterminate wilderness. State leaders believed that there needed to be a buffer zone between the new American cities and a variety of forces opposed to this new country. So legislation was passed in 1786 that drew a developer's grid of civilization upon the land, dividing the space into large tracts, each with systematically derived subdivisions. A year later the first large chunk of those tracts, still nothing more than discursive images agreed upon by legislators, were sold at auction in a New York City coffeehouse to an Irish fur trader out of Detroit named Alexander Macomb. With that act, the drive to contain and manage this wilderness began. But it would take another decade before that conceptual grid would be cut into the land.

In the summer of 1799, two teams of men set out from the edge of the known world to undertake the daunting task of surveying Macomb's Purchase. In particular, these men were to delineate ten towns, new places already labeled with Old World names like Lisbon, Canton, Potsdam, and Madrid. The teams, one group of twenty men headed by Benjamin Wright and another of eleven headed by his cousin Moses

Wright, were to rendezvous along the shores of the St. Lawrence some miles downriver from where Lake Ontario transforms itself into the great river. The latter group, however, was delayed. The subsequent journey of Moses and his men illustrates the world in which Abner Powell and his family lived six years later.[5]

While Benjamin's team traveled via bateau from Oneida Lake northward toward the St. Lawrence, Moses's team left from an interior location and therefore needed to hike through the forest for days to reach the designated meeting place, a small, crude cabin that was the only structure known in all the region. When the overland group finally arrived at the spot, they discovered not their compatriots but a letter stating that Benjamin's team had waited for several days and then decided to proceed to the settlement of St. Regis, eighty miles downriver to the northeast. By this time Moses and his men were in trouble. They had little food left and no bateau to get them downriver. Rationing their meager provisions, they tore apart the cabin, rebuilt it in the form of a raft, and set out for St. Regis.

Some miles downriver they came upon a group of men cutting trees on the New York side of the river. Moses and his team soon discovered that these men were timber thieves from Upper Canada who were transporting the trees across to the northern shore. It was these smugglers who provided the means necessary—food and boats—to enable the group to make it to the Canadian river village of Brockville and then on to the mouth of the Oswegatchie River, where they found Benjamin and his men.

Here was one important lesson: know your enemies but befriend them if you can. There were no rules, just survival.

America in 1799 was in the midst of its first cold war: the British continued to harass American ships and outposts even though the War of Independence had been concluded and its peace treaty ratified by Congress in January 1784. The two countries were continually threatening each other and sometimes even trading hostilities. A dozen years later the cold war would ignite into the War of 1812 and last for two and a half years. These instabilities, coupled with the young country's daunting internal struggle to define itself—a struggle that threatened to split the country east to west or north to south—made line drawing both important and problematic.[6]

Regardless of the boundaries drawn by politicians, generals, and their cartographers, regardless of this faith in their ability to delineate sovereignties by proclamation, on the ground these distinctions were often negotiable or muddied. So, for example, one might find that Canadian smugglers, ostensibly loyal to the British Empire, stole from its enemy to the south while giving sustenance to that same enemy, Moses and his men, even as the latter were on a quest to lay claim to the land the Canadians were exploiting.

It was this type of ambivalence that governed Abner Powell as he set out for the river. While he was on his way to meet men across the border, forces at the highest level of government were beginning to constrict the relationship between the United States and British-held Upper Canada. President Jefferson was drafting a warning to Great Britain to stop harassing America's trading vessels. Jefferson was soon to ask for and receive the initial legislation limiting the rights of Americans to trade with the British. Although Powell could not know it at the time, what he was contemplating would soon be in violation of his nation's trade laws. But then again, federal laws, even state laws, were far removed from the demands of the frontier.

Powell left his daughter after assuring her that if she'd keep a watch out, by sundown she would spy him and Mr. Bear coming across the field. And if he had a good day, he told her with a wink, she'd see him dragging a skidder with a deer on it. So she stayed out to watch him trudge along the edge of the snowfield until he disappeared into the cut toward the river.

For Powell it was a relief to get into the woods. The temperature had been dropping since the snowstorm passed through the night before and the rising wind had made his walk difficult along the field's frozen, white expanse, a stretch of land that had been tentatively fertile six months before and so dark and dense the year before that. This field was Powell's wealth, his lifeline. After clearing it a year ago with the help of his two oldest sons, Powell had had a modest but promising summer growing corn and assorted vegetables that fed the family and their few livestock. In addition, the Powells, like the few other pioneer farmers in the region, built a small log house and a small barn, and made all their hand tools; they split cedar trees for fencing, fashioned wooden buckets and taps to collect the early spring maple sap, and hunted whatever game they could to keep themselves alive. If they could survive the winter, they would continue to cut the trees and till the soil. And this prospect was at the center of Powell's plan to go beyond mere subsistence living. After winter, he hoped to produce something new: he'd cut more trees, burn over the new clearing, collect the ashes, boil them in kettles, and dry them out to create potash, the "black salts" used for fertilizer, soap, gunpowder, and explosives. If he and his neighbors could do this on a large enough scale, they might be able to start selling potash to others.[7]

Like many of his compatriots who ventured into Macomb's Purchase, Powell and his wife, Elizabeth, had migrated west from Vermont and the Powell family farm to buy land in this "new" territory, a tract that was only now opening up to settlers. In the years leading up to the Revolution, this land had been under the watch of the British navy. In the intervening years after the war, New York had used its increasing powers over the ever-weakening Haudenosaunee to lay claim to this land in treaty after treaty. By the turn of the century, these appropriations appeared to be nearly complete and the state wanted this land to be settled. But up here there would be no giveaways of land to lure the homesteaders as there would be across much of the fledgling nation. In New York there would be commerce and entrepreneurs. The state would sell vast parcels of land to developers, who in turn would work to recoup their investments by selling properties to potential settlers. Dabbling in north country land speculation at this time were a number of wealthy, well-known figures, including Alexander Hamilton, John Jay, and William Cooper, the father of James Fennimore Cooper.[8] Yet by the time Powell arrived only a thousand or so adventurers had braved the extreme weather, difficult access and terrain, and short growing season to sprinkle themselves and their tree-cutting agendas across this wilderness expanse. Land was cheap and plentiful but money was scarce. Perhaps if they could produce more than they consumed, the great river would be a means by which they could distribute their surplus.[9]

On his way down to the river, Powell realized that despite the storm, the snow was spotty in the woods. At this elevation, it usually wasn't snow that was the driving force of winter, it was the cold. The deep snow was usually to the south and up into the highlands, the extreme cold to the north and down into the great river valley. On this morning, however, there should be enough cover to track game, and Powell and five companions, three Americans and two Canadians, would meet on the north side of the river to hunt deer. But these men had another agenda as well. They wanted to discuss a deal to move resources back and forth and then down the river. Under some circumstances this was called trading, under others, smuggling.

The four Americans were to meet at the landing in Louisville, where there would be an old dugout canoe large enough for ten men. Today they would travel light so there would be room for the kill they hoped to bring back. As Powell and Mr. Bear neared the river he could see color through the trees. It wasn't hard to spot, a patch of red moving across the pewter gray sky and river. That would be his neighboring farmer, Alexander. And soon they would meet Barber and Chapman, both of whom had traveled from the village of Madrid during the snowstorm the day before and had found a room in Wilson's public house near the landing.

These four men had been meeting when time allowed since the late fall, occasionally with their families—a group that totaled over twenty—for a festive meal or small celebration of one kind or another, but mostly to hunt and talk about how to improve their lots. All of them had come to this outpost in search of lucrative land. Barber had been trained in medicine in Boston and had been lured to Macomb's Purchase by the opportunity to buy a large piece of land at a very low price—land he subsequently leased out for farming while he set himself up as the first physician in the region. Like Powell, Alexander and Chapman sought their fortunes in small farms that they hoped would grow larger and larger.

At the landing the men exchanged greetings and helped one another with their provisions. For Powell, and, he suspected, for the others too, these meetings were not only enjoyable for the good companionship, they also bolstered his confidence in his ability to survive. Powell faced many days when he wondered if he should have brought his family to this rough place. Sometimes though, when he expressed doubts to Elizabeth, she would remind him how unhappy they had been the years before they set out on this adventure. As the third son, married with a young family and working on his father's farm, Powell had chafed at a future in which the best he could hope for was to be employed by his father or one of his older brothers. As the children came one by one, he and Elizabeth talked more and more about setting off on their own. When their two sons were old enough to handle the work, the westward journey was begun.

Still, it never left him that he and Elizabeth were only a thin line of defense between his children, their fortune, and the forces opposing them: the hard land, the weather, the wolves, and the Others, whoever they may be, who wanted to take their land. But on the odd day when he could hunt and scheme with his counterparts, he'd be reminded that they all faced the same doubts and difficulties. If they could sustain their own families, maybe they could help one another and, in turn, the community could sustain all of them.

"The crossing looks advantageous now," said one of the men, and the rest agreed. With their gear loaded and Mr. Bear standing at the bow, the men pushed the canoe across the icy shelf that clung to the shore before boarding the vessel, poling over the final icy stretch, and then sliding out into the mild current. The wind gusted occasionally but the swells were small. As they paddled in unison, they kept the bow at an angle to the waves, bumping up occasionally against the odd chunk of floating ice.

The river here could be crossed throughout the year if one was careful. From the landing one could maneuver around two islands, Cat's Island on the west, and on the east, a much larger island that eventually became known as Croil's. Once past the islands it was a straight line across the open water to the north shore. Though rough at times, this stretch of water was nothing like the Long Sault Rapids just downriver from the landing. The Long Sault section was one of the most treacher-

ous stretches in the entire length of the river, from its Lake
Ontario source to its mouth in the North Atlantic.

While Haudenosaunee canoeists had traveled the river in
its natural state for eons, some of the earliest Europeans visitors, with their technologically based drive to alter the natural
landscape, sought to change the river's navigability by digging
small locks and canals designed to skirt rapids in one stretch or
another. The earliest known effort dated back to 1700, when
French explorers attempted to build a canal a mile long, twelve
feet wide, and eighteen inches deep along the Lachine Rapids
near the early settlement of Montreal.[10] Since then such projects had been attempted on and off in a variety of locations. To
many explorers, settlers, traders, entrepreneurs, military leaders, and politicians, the great river looked like the means to
make men rich—if they could just get their goods in large
enough quantities through the river as quickly as possible. For
such men, the river promised speed and access that rivaled any
other means of transportation or communication. At a time
and place when overland travel was slow and laborious, before
railroads and before the telegraph, rivers offered high-speed
movement of materials and information. The St. Lawrence
and its large tributaries were becoming the backbone to a network of nodes, including the shoreline settlements as well as
those patches of cleared land at the end of primitive roads
carved through the forests. If the rivers could be made navigable, if they could carry away the timber and other resources to
pay for the cutting of roads and the building of villages along
their shores, if an infrastructure of laws and economy could
follow systematically from these activities, then there was the
potential for large-scale exploitation of new commercial resources and markets in the interior continent. This hope fueled the drive to increase the river's capacity.

Out where the current picked up, Powell spied two figures on the northern shore. That would have been Campbell and his friend, a man Powell knew only as the Surveyor, so named because he had worked on the great project begun by Benjamin and Moses Wright on the American side six years before. Despite their different allegiances, these Canadians and their families were compatriots in survival with the south shore men. The farmers on the north were mostly the sons and daughters of British loyalist exiles from the Hudson and Mohawk valleys who had fled north during the war. Thirty years later, local circumstances rendered the next generation freer to ignore that history.

The Americans negotiated the canoe to a spot along the northern shore where the ice had given way. They landed, greeted their hosts, and prepared for a day of hunting. After securing the canoe, the group began the trek to a parcel of forest known for the thick foraging possibilities it offered the native deer. It would be hard work to ferret out the game but a small group could do it, four of them driving the animals toward two shooters. Later the men would reconnoiter to discuss the other matter of business: their tentative plan to develop potash and transport it downriver to potential buyers. As these six men laughed and helped one another with the task at hand, only those with great foresight could have imagined that half a dozen years later, after the formal declaration of the next war, a meeting like this would need to happen in secret.

During the early months of that war, in the summer of 1812, men on both sides of the river were conscripted into the military and taken off to forts and campaigns some distances away. Many would never return. But for those left behind, the challenges of self-preservation in this daunting climate hadn't changed at all. These people knew that survival meant cooperating with one another, helping one another, complementing one another's labors. And for those years between the arrival of the first surveyors and the declaration of war, settlers on both sides, like the six hunters, acted as though they were one community, traveling often back and forth both for friendship and for profit. But at the outset of the war, this travel was curtailed, if not obliterated. Even though there may have been no hostilities between these friends, the war began to change the way people thought of one another: perhaps these people across the way were indeed their enemy despite their rich and cooperative recent past. Perhaps they did need to watch out for the Other across the river. Six years after Powell crossed the river to meet his Canadian neighbors, contact between Louisville and the northern shore became tentative and wary; the time was tense.

Early one summer during the hostilities an American who lived along the shore in Louisville became disgusted with his neighbors, who seemed to him to be too passive in light of the declaration of war. He may have feared that a roving British company would think the south shore unprotected and ripe for plunder, so he decided with a couple of accomplices that he would trick his neighbors on the north side, now enemies, into thinking that the Americans were readying for war. On a lovely, quiet June evening, these conspirators built a number of fires on points viewable from the north and then began to move along the shoreline yelling out orders, as if they were commanding troops who were taking up positions along the shore. The call and response of the phony commander and his officers echoed across the river. The purpose was merely to announce to the Canadians that the south shore was protected. But the display had a far greater effect.

As the conspirators had hoped, the fires were noticed in Upper Canada. Likewise, the shouts were heard and understood to be the arrival of American troops on the border. With dogs barking and a general alarm sounded, the Canadians along the shore, fearing that an attack was imminent, fled on foot and in wagons back into the thickets of woods, where they spent the night terrified of what violence was coming. Soon after, word of this threat reached some British commanders, and a battalion descended on Louisville ready for combat. This time it was the American farmers scurrying to hide in the thick woods, fearing for their lives. When the British found no opposition, they set off downriver. And tentatively, one by one, the Americans returned to their homes along the shore, very unhappy with the false firebrand among them.[11]

It wasn't long, however, before the people of Louisville decided that, even though many of their young men had been drafted into armed service, it would be prudent for those who remained to defend the community. So that summer the settlers of Louisville organized a small militia of about forty men to protect their stretch of the south shore, and they nominated one of their company to command the group as high sergeant. Word of this militia reached the American military command upriver in Ogdensburg, and General Jacob Brown sent orders for the Louisville men to stop every boat that passed their shores in order to learn the voyageurs' business and inspect their cargo. Occasionally a boat carrying strategic supplies was intercepted and the cargo confiscated. Such efforts, of course, were not without their dangers.

The following January, seven years after Abner Powell and his companions set out for a hunting trip in Upper Canada, a man from the north shore who knew the south shore well, who had worked as a surveyor years before, crossed the river to recover goods commandeered by the Americans. Reuben Sherwood, a captain in the British army but known and respected among those on the south side, led a small company of loyalists as they braved the January night crossing and landed on a point upriver from Louisville, a few miles from where Powell's party had begun their trip.

Sherwood posted guards among the locals to dampen their resistance and commandeered several wagons and teams and rode some miles to a storage building where the confiscated provisions had been held. The captain, out of respect for his former neighbors, harmed no one, but resolutely marched his troops back to the river and their boats by the break of day and crossed back to the north. As the party began to navigate through the treacherous winter waters, a band of Americans organized to make chase; however, they discovered on the shore a quantity of drink, a liquor called shrub left by Sherwood's party in plain sight. After the pursuing band stopped to sample the drink, they decided that Sherwood and his men were too far ahead and the river too dangerous to continue the pursuit. They would, however, exact a measure of revenge by finishing off the liquor.[12]

With events like these, the Louisville farmers and their families became fearful of imminent incursions from their former neighbors. They became vigilant and suspicious. Border crossings dwindled and what was a difficult life became a bit meaner. That first year of the war grew particularly trying for the families on the northern shore. With most men gone to the British garrison thirty miles upriver in the loyalist village of Prescott, the remaining settlers found themselves low on provisions. Finally, one night the children of one family, remembering the close relations they had had with families on the south shore and having the confidence to navigate the river at night, crossed over and found their way to the house of former friends. They knocked on the door and begged the Americans for help, for food. The response was overwhelming. The Louisville family was joyful at the prospect of helping their friends and this act began the process of reconnecting families on both sides of the shore. Although these contacts were kept hidden from officials, they quietly flourished and spread among the river settlers. The lines of war that had been drawn were thus undermined. The governments along the river were enemies; the people, a community. Peace was declared on this frontier long before it was declared in the opposing capitals.

"Share and share alike" were the words Campbell used when the men discussed how the hunt would proceed. The first deer kill should go south of the border, suggested Campbell, the second north. If they were fortunate beyond that, they could decide then how to divvy up the remainder. So the men agreed that one north shore man and one south shore man would set up as shooters while the other four would drive. Given the increasingly strong wind out of the east, it was decided that the shooters would take a position on the western edge of the forest. With the Surveyor leading the way, the shooters would need to proceed along a small, rocky, meandering stream—a difficult trek—for about a mile, take not the first branch but the second branch on the left, and keep rock hopping until they found a stretch of forest with a good view back toward the east. From there the men would separate and dig in. Powell's name was offered by one of the others but he quickly said no and suggested that his neighbor Alexander, a good shot, take on the task. Besides, Powell added, he had brought his dog expressly for the purpose of driving and they would all be better off if he directed his animal in the drive. Barber and Chapman agreed and Alexander left with the Surveyor to follow the trail to the designated spot.

Despite his reputation as an excellent shot, Powell declined the opportunity for a very specific reason, one he did not wish to reveal to his companions. It was not because of the dog; any of his countrymen could have kept Mr. Bear to the task. It was not out of laziness; no one among his neighbors worked longer or harder than he. Nor did he shirk responsibility; Powell had readily taken on difficult communal tasks in the past and believed them necessary for their mutual survival. And he didn't decline out of some sort of polite modesty; he had proven his marksman's skills to these men a number of times and he had never shied away from their praises. No, Powell chose not to take up the shooting position because of a simple but profound fear he suffered, one he had never spoken of aloud but that he recognized well. He feared getting lost in the woods. For all the adventuring a man like Powell had experienced in seeking his fortune on this frontier, for all the hundreds of miles he had traveled along the edges of this little-known land, Powell feared losing his way in the wilderness. It had to do with geography and family history. And it drove him to clear fields and cut paths, to connect his property to others' and to help build a village because that was the only defense against the forces of destruction.

When Powell was a young child, but not too young to remember, his family had escaped a vicious, terrifying raid by a British-led party of Haudenosaunee who had made an incursion into the interior farmlands of Vermont in search of provisions and hostages. In the fall of 1780, the raiding party attacked the Vermont towns of Randolph, Royalton, Sharon, and Tunbridge, looting, burning homes and barns, killing livestock, and taking prisoners, especially those who could be used as bargaining chips in the British and American conflict.[13] Powell's family—his parents, his two older brothers, three sisters, and a cousin—had been alerted to trouble by several warning shots that must have come from some miles away. They were lucky enough to get off the farm, into the woods, and down into a particularly deep and wet ravine, where they spent two nights huddled together before venturing out.

What they and a handful of other survivors found was utter devastation—their cows shot or hacked to death, their barns burned to the ground. Unlike others, however, the Powells' house had not been burned; the reason why was unclear. But everything in it had been either stolen or destroyed. The family and their remaining neighbors worked together to make it through the winter, but Powell's father had seen enough. After speaking with some men in the nearby village, Powell Sr. left, midwinter, for several weeks and when he returned, he announced that the family was moving to a more advantageous location, one where they would have a better line of sight and less to fear. His father had entered into an agreement to purchase land to the northwest of Randolph on the edge of the great valley of Lake Champlain. In addition, he had purchased enough parts to build a new wagon to transport all that they had left. The family would move as soon as the weather improved. So a month later, before the spring thaw would make the road too muddy for the wagon, but late enough so that all could survive the coldest temperatures, the family moved to a new patch of land. As the crow flies, this new place wasn't more than thirty miles to the west. But it lay on the other side of a very difficult mountain range and the trip around it was twice as far.

Although Powell Sr. had purchased enough acreage to include some of the valley floor, the family began clearing the upper reaches of their property, where the land was drier and potentially more tillable. It was there that Abner Powell was raised, high up on the side of a mountain with a view of a vast and open valley, and it was there that he was taught to maintain long views and good sight lines because then one could spot trouble long before it arrived. Far to the west was the endless mountain wilderness of New York. To the north and to the south, the lake and its tributaries and all of the flat fertile land around them stretched beyond the bounds of sight. If any party had designs on this farm, it would be spied for days before it even got close. The only way to surprise the Powells would be to come from the east over the top of the mountain, and that would be a daunting task for anyone.

As Abner Powell grew up he spent countless hours in the surrounding woods, but he rarely entered areas that he or a companion didn't already know well; nor did he often leave the higher elevations replete with sporadic openings and rock faces that offered panoramic views of the land before him. On those occasions when he ventured deep into the lower woods, he became noticeably ill at ease. Several times he got disoriented despite his efforts to concentrate on the key signs: the location of the sun, the patterns of growth on the trees, and such. Usually this happened when he was out by himself hunting. But once he and a companion got terribly lost and spent the night huddled in a makeshift shelter before following a spring brook that eventually connected to a larger stream which he correctly guessed would intersect with a trail he knew.

Yet even though his inclination was to avoid the wilderness, he often found himself wondering as he worked on the farm what adventures there might be among the great blue mountain ranges that rose far across the valley. Part of this fascination was spurred by the danger inherent in that rough land. There were always stories circulating about unusually massive bears or long, deadly waterfalls that suddenly appeared as one explorer or another navigated a seemingly placid stream. And yes, those mountains were still hunting grounds for the Haudenosaunee and that fact alone struck fear in many white settlers. But despite the terrifying raid on Randolph, Powell didn't fear the Haudenosaunee. As he grew up, he came to know a few who traveled around the valley. And from what he could learn, it seemed as though just as many Haudenosaunee were allied with the Americans as were with the British. It was the British who caused the most concern. The tales of captives who survived the British prisoner of war camps in Canada were truly horrific. The torture and depravity in those places made it easy to believe that the captors were allied with Satan himself, because certainly no God-fearing human could inflict such suffering.

Powell knew that his family's mountain farm was as safe a place as could be in these frontier lands. So why didn't he and Elizabeth just stay in their aerie, perched above the dangers and uncertainties below and beyond? Because another force moved them and many others like them: a drive to create their own fortune. Land was the one path to this goal available to the common man—if he could get some and make it productive. For the third son, the Vermont farm was not a place where this could happen. But in the first decade of the new century there was another option, and that's what led him one spring to travel with his own sons north up Lake Champlain to a crude trail that served as the only path west to a place called Chateaugay, then to the St. Lawrence River and eventually to a dense, low-lying land with no panoramic outlooks from which to see danger approaching.[14]

Suddenly Mr. Bear bolted off to the right. Just as Powell turned he saw one white tail flashing, then two more, then another, and another. The drive was on. For the next hour the four men, spreading out as far as they could without losing sight of one another, moved forward methodically across a difficult terrain fraught with blow-downs and thickets. The wind gusts had gotten so loud that Powell barely heard the first shot.

He clearly heard the second. A few minutes later, two more. Cradling his weapon in his arms, Powell waited attentively until he heard a call in the distance and he knew the hunt was done. After several calls and responses Powell found his way to where Alexander was kneeling over a carcass, slicing it up through its abdomen to clean it. Not more than fifty yards away, the Surveyor disemboweled another.

These deer were of the same population that had helped sustain the Haudenosaunee for generations. Now there was increasing competition from a different hunter. Over many years the relations between the white settlers and the Haudenosaunee had been complex and changing, involving shifting loyalties, exploitation, outright theft of lands, war, terrorism, abduction, treaties imposed, treaties broken, comradeship against common enemies, a sharing of knowledge about the land and its living creatures, and fundamentally different views of man's relationship to that land and those creatures. But the one clear outcome of it all was the unrelenting appropriation of the Haudenosaunee's vast hunting and fishing grounds by the white settlers.

When Benjamin and Moses Wright and their surveying teams set out reunited from the Oswegatchie River on that summer day in 1799, their goal was to reach the Haudenosaunee village of St. Regis, about fifteen miles downriver from the spot that would become Louisville Landing. There they would assemble and proceed in an orderly fashion to cut into Macomb's Purchase the lines demarcating the towns the state had mandated into existence. When the surveyors' boats approached the Long Sault Rapids, some of the party became afraid and decided to put to shore and go overland along the river. But these men encountered obstacles on that route, and when they reached the Grasse River and came upon some

Haudenosaunee traveling down the St. Lawrence, they hired these men to transport them downriver, eventually to St. Regis. At first the residents of the village became alarmed as they realized that different groups of white men were approaching. They organized an armed resistance to defend their lives and property. But after much negotiation, the Haudenosaunee decided that these men meant no harm and graciously accepted them into their village.[15]

With the technologies of surveying, with their axes and chains, those men who came in peace ended the wilderness forever. They may not have borne arms, but their work imposed the white man's patterns on the land and that incursion would be more profound and far-reaching than any armed incursion ever could. Within that first year the first road was cut from St. Regis along the river to Louisville and the first settler, Nahum Wilson, settled near Louisville Landing. Within two years the rivers that flow north into the St. Lawrence—the Raquette, Grasse, St. Regis, and Oswegatchie—were explored, camps established, and the towns demarcated. And although the surveyors and early settlers constantly faced starvation and a variety of other dangers, it wasn't long before the mills were built, the forests began to fall, and the white men began to make their fortunes.[16]

In 1806 a person could make money a variety of ways from cutting wood. Like Powell, one could farm the cleared land. One could mill the wood and sell lumber. One could burn the wood and make charcoal to fire stoves and furnaces—furnaces that over time grew larger and larger: in 1830 it was figured that one factory furnace in Syracuse used two hundred thousand cords of wood per year for charcoal, requiring the yearly burning of three thousand acres of northern for-

est.[17] Or one could burn the wood to make potash, which
would be profitable if one could amass enough of it.

This latter proposition was what the men discussed on
their way out of the woods—a difficult trip made even more
so by the effort required to carry out the carcasses. Several of
them had heard from a variety of people passing on the river
that there might soon be restrictions on trade across this border. Campbell recounted a story he had heard about a man
named Jacob Brown upriver in Ogdensburg, who had a going
concern moving quantities of potash across the border and
who openly claimed that he would keep doing so no matter
what restrictions were placed on trade. It was apparently worth
the risk, Campbell told them, because potash might bring a
hundred dollars or more a ton.[18]

By the time the group reached the shoreline, the day's light
was waning and the swells on the river were unusually high.
The wind was almost constant now and crossing would be
quite risky. After some discussion the Americans decided to
load the canoe with their quarry and equipment but wait until
after sunset to set out. Perhaps by then the wind would
weaken. While Campbell and the Surveyor departed for their
homes, the four Americans repaired to a small, crude lean-to a
little ways off the shoreline, where they continued to discuss
the means necessary to get into the potash trade, legally or ille-
gally. They speculated about the amount of land they'd need to
burn, what other advantageous forest tracts might be available
and at what price, how they might make the collection and
production of the ash as efficient as possible, how they could
transport quantities, and who might be interested in buying
from them.

For these men in this place at this time, there was no clear
intersection of law and commerce. In a young nation with

ever-changing boundaries and fiercely competitive commercial interests, trying to establish its legitimacy and sovereignty in a dangerous world, the rule of law needed to be marked and noted. It needed to become something one could see and touch. Another decade would pass before that marker would be set in this place.

Across the river and ten years after those four men sat together in the lean-to laying out a plan to make more money than any of them had ever earned before, Louis Gerteau carried the ax into the lumberman's house and committed his horrific crime. Where the murderer's captors stood might still have been called a frontier, but it was no longer a wilderness. Gerteau did not suffer rough justice on the spot but instead was taken into custody to stand trial. On July 12, 1816, in the village of Ogdensburg in front of a huge crowd of citizens, Louis Gerteau, found guilty the week before during official proceedings in the county courthouse, was hanged by the neck until dead, the first man to suffer the death penalty by law in this new land.[19]

Within twenty years of the time the Wrights and their surveying teams had set out on their task, an infrastructure was in place: the towns envisioned by the state were settled, forests were bisected, roads were cut, rivers were being transformed from natural, capricious flows into a reliable, industrious network for moving information and materials, communities were evolving, the agrarian economy had gone beyond mere self-sufficiency, and the rule of law had eked its way across this land, connecting responsibilities to freedoms, individuals to groups, outpost to outpost, settlement to settlement, bringing even these far reaches into the pulsing grid that binds villages, counties, states, and country. At the turn of the nineteenth century, to live on the shores of this northern frontier was to be connected, for good or for ill, to something larger than just

one's locality; it meant being connected to an economy, a
state, a nation.

If they could just survive the wind, the cold, and the ice.

It was the ice that first gave Powell a start. A sheet several
feet across scraped by the canoe shortly after the men finally set
out on the return crossing. On this night it was nearly impossible to see these blocks: black, submerged, punishing. Perhaps
they were breaking off from the large ice sheet that bridged
both shores some lengths upriver. Powell commanded the dog
to lie down and tied him tightly to an iron hook in the bow.
He didn't want a jumpy animal to cause problems. But it didn't
work out as he had planned. Powell had no vantage point from
which to spy his enemy at a distance. Out past Cat's and Croil's
Islands, as the four men strained to keep the canoe at a stable
angle to the waves, something—perhaps another jarring colli-
sion with a sheet of ice—made the dog jump and flail at a particularly bad moment, a moment when the swells placed the
canoe on the edge of a precipice. And over it all went into the
raging black shock of the numbing river.

Franklin Hough recounted the moment fifty years later:

They had been over to Canada, where they were de-
tained by the roughness of the river, occasioned by a
strong east wind, which always produces a swell, from
its encountering the current. Towards night, the wind
having abated, they attempted to cross in a log canoe,
but their boat capsized, and two of their number are
supposed to have drowned immediately. The other
two clung to their boat, and endeavored, by cries, to
obtain assistance. These cries were heard on both
shores of the river, and to a great distance below, as
they floated down; but no one paid any particular at-

tention to them, not realizing that they proceeded
from persons in distress, and they all perished. Three of
the bodies were found several miles below; but the
fourth at a great distance below, among the islands. A
large dog who was aboard had been bound to keep
him quiet, and is supposed to have overturned them.
This sad accident spread gloom through the settlement, and was a cause of unavailing regret to those
who had heard the cries, without hastening to their
assistance. No blame was attached to any one, and the
darkness of the night, and roughness of the river, were
such, that aid could scarcely have been afforded, had
the situation of the sufferers been appreciated.[20]

Sometime between the years 1799 and 1815 a Haudenosaunee teacher named Handsome Lake sought a way to
find a moral middle path for his people to follow between the
traditions of the past and the ways of the white men who had
taken so much of the native hunting lands. Drawing on the
wisdom of spiritual messengers, Handsome Lake taught that
"three things that our younger brethren [the white people] do
are right to follow."

Now, the first. The white man works on a tract of
cultivated ground and harvests food for his family. So
if he should die they still have the ground for help. If
any of your people have cultivated ground let them
not be proud on that account. If one is proud there is
sin within him but if there be no pride there is no sin.

Now, the second thing. It is the way a white man
builds a house. He builds one warm and fine appearing so if he dies the family has the house for help.
Whoso among you does this does right, always pro-

viding there is no pride. If there is pride it is evil but if there is none, it is well.

Now, the third. The white man keeps horses and cattle. Now there is no evil in this for they are a help to his family. So if he dies his family has the stock for help. Now all this is right if there is no pride. No evil will follow this practice if the animals are well fed, treated kindly and not overworked. Tell this to your people.[21]

Families were the first defense against destruction. But for families to outlast any one of their members, they needed to build their infrastructures—their fields, their homes, their livestock—and link them together by river, road, and village. If such connections could be made on the shores of the St. Lawrence, then the families of Louisville Landing would survive.

That night, as she waited for her father's return, Amanda Powell ventured out onto the porch and into the cold. She pulled a blanket tightly around herself and looked out past the barn and across the fields toward the cut in the woods. She thought she heard the cow stirring for a moment as if the dog was about. Then all was quiet again, even the wind. Her mother called to her but she waited just a moment before opening the door and returning to the warming fire inside.

the grid crumbles

thursday, january 8, 1998

In the darkness, half-asleep, I imagined sudden violence. Trees, ice, wind—something—hurtling down at extreme velocities to rip open an old wound, rending another jagged hole where the fire had burned, tearing open the scar of guilt ("How could we have let the fire happen?") that had been covered over with plywood and Tyvek and vinyl siding. Or, even more plausibly, some force at any moment would shatter the large window fitted into the wall where the chimney had once been and radiate across our bed shards of glass. And this time we wouldn't be so lucky. Catastrophe would hit us while we slept, or tried to, and undo all the reconstruction that had turned near tragedy into nothing more traumatic than a remodeling spree. Yet, despite the gusting wind and chattering, creaking trees, all that was happening for the moment was the slow accretion that occurs when water carried aloft thousands of miles from warmer climes descends onto a crystalline landscape: cold, white, and brittle.

Our dogs were restless. First one then another climbed onto the bed and then quickly jumped off. In a short while another jumped back on and stood panting, shaking the bed. I faded in and out of sleep to the sound of clicking: ice in the trees and dog toenails back and forth across the floor, out into the hallway, back in, back out, around and around. At some point in the wee hours I noticed the absence of the red LED numbers of the clock radio. Maybe the power will be back by morning, I said to myself.

Several miles away in his village apartment, North Country Public Radio reporter Mitch Teich learned that his electricity would not be on in the morning. Just before 3 A.M. he was awakened by a crash outside his bedroom window. A conduit running up the side of the building and housing its electric service wires had just been ripped off the outside wall and lay sparking in the frozen mess below. There was nothing to do about it, so Mitch went back to sleep.

By then Mike Weil was awake and thinking that maybe the contingency plans he and the other Potsdam officials had drawn up the night before would be necessary after all. At three-thirty he drove over to the village fire station and began discussing those plans with several other emergency response personnel.

At that point most roads were merely ice-covered but that was changing. Trees and lines were beginning to fall at a faster rate and within a couple of hours conditions had worsened noticeably across the north country. At five-thirty Al Bradley and his crews were heading back out from the Malone NiMo center forty miles to the east when Al ran into one of the local Malone line crews returning from a night's work. Al recognized the foreman, who told Al about the work the crew had done that night on the main highway that was across the north country. "I've never seen anything like this in all my life," he said. "I just cut Route 11. A path on Route 11 from Malone to Moira," a distance of about twelve to fifteen miles. "All I did was cut wires and poles out of the way for the rescue squad. I didn't put anything up. I didn't get anyone back on power. I didn't set any poles. I didn't fix a goddamn thing. I spent all night trying to get that rescue squad to Moira. Every pole was down. Every single one of them." The man looked at Al. "It's terrible out there," he said.

These two men and their crews, whether they knew it or not, were early participants in what was quickly evolving into a reconstruction project of unprecedented size and scope. As Al returned to the storm, NiMo managers in Syracuse were busy establishing the overall emergency response to the unfolding damage. In its Northern Regional Control Center the storm director and his staff had set up a management structure to battle the storm and prioritized the work to be done. They would split the affected area into two sectors, the Watertown region to the west and the St. Lawrence to the north. In each sector the service centers would be fully staffed so that decisions could be made and enacted in the field. Both the Potsdam and Malone centers, for example, would operate with the full contingent of personnel necessary to restore power in their respective areas.

The first task in every area was to keep the transmission grid operating. Power comes into a grid from a variety of sources and flows toward the demand. In New York power flows from west to east and from north to south. The major power generation sources in Niagara Falls and south central Ontario flow toward urban centers like Rochester, Syracuse, Albany, and New York City. Flowing to those destinations from the north is power generated by the massive hydro dams in Quebec as well as the Moses-Saunders Power Dam on the St. Lawrence Seaway.

All of this power energizes a network made up of large transmission loops. For example, Potsdam is part of a loop that connects to the Canadian grid in the north and circles around to connect to other loops in the east, south, and west. Such a design enables power to move from any source to any point along the loop. So if, for example, a connection to the west is lost, the rest of the loop can be energized by sources from the north or by simply rerouting western power in the opposite direction to reach the southern and eastern connections. Loops offer redundancies that seemingly ensure a fail-safe connection to other energized segments of the regional and national power grids.

By now, however, the redundancies in this regional loop were beginning to fail. Several hours earlier, around the time the conduit was falling off Mitch Teich's apartment building, transmission lines to the south had fallen, eliminating one of two major southern connections. About ten minutes later, towers in the north had crumbled, dropping out one of the connections to power generated on the St. Lawrence Seaway and further north in Quebec.

At home the poles were still standing but the trees were crumbling, and that's what spooked the dogs. On any other day when I'd open the door in the early morning darkness, they'd scoot out anxious to trace the rabbit and chipmunk trails. But this morning only the younger lab, Ry, seemed unconcerned; the other two I couldn't get out the door. It didn't help that a branch fell from the top of a sixty-foot aspen and landed twenty-five feet from the back door just as I tried to push one of them out. Finally, I picked up Gerta, the dog most likely to use the downstairs carpet in place of the great outdoors, and carried her through the garage and out an open pass door that was frozen in place next to the bays. I struggled to keep ahold of her as I gingerly stepped across an open field next to the house. All around us we heard the constant chattering of ice punctuated by intermittent gunshots of breaking branches. About thirty yards out into the field I let Gerta down. Immediately she ran away from me and disappeared back through the pass door. Ry was sniffing around my feet when I saw an orange flash on the horizon, a fiery flare somewhere in the village. A few seconds later another. Ry went on alert at the sound of alarm in my voice. A moment later a brilliant blue explosion lit up the entire dome of the sky. I ducked involuntarily and Ry skittered away from me. A mile away on the other side of the river, Mike Warden, Lynn's son, had just opened his eyes when the world outside his bedroom window was suddenly revealed in that silent flash of light. In that moment he could see as clearly as if it was midday but under a sickly green sun. His wife, Marge, slept on, the baby due in little more than a week.

As soon as I got back in the house I told Kath that the flashed made it look like we just got nuked. I also reported that things looked pretty bad out there and it might be a few hours before we got our power back. By then she had already found our camping cookstove and begun boiling water for coffee. I went off in search of batteries for a portable radio and on the way I checked the inside temperature. Fifty-five upstairs, probably a few degrees colder down. Not too bad. Maybe all the insulation we had added during the fire reconstruction would pay off, especially if it took most of the day to get our power back.

How long this would all last was the key question facing Mike Weil and his colleagues as they began speaking with local Red Cross officials at 6 A.M. Working out of the Potsdam Fire Station, which was energized by a generator running only a radio and a couple of lights, the Potsdam officials had decided to set up an emergency shelter at SUNY Potsdam, and the physical plant people there were already opening up the field house, Maxcy Hall, for that purpose. How big should it be? How many people might need the shelter? These were the issues that Mike; Bob White, a county deputy fire coordinator;

and Chris Taylor, Potsdam's assistant fire chief, discussed as they spoke with the Red Cross. Early on it had been decided that the assistant chief would manage the fire company response because the chief also served as the town highway superintendent and he was busy managing road maintenance.

The Red Cross rep first said that they could get thirty cots to three different locations in the county: Gouverneur, Potsdam, and Massena. Mike and the others talked about this and decided that if thirty was all they would need, then there was no real disaster. But if the situation was truly serious they would need far more. "So what do you think? How many?" the Red Cross rep asked. "How about three hundred?" asked Mike.

"You know," the rep said with a note of caution, "I just talked with Red Cross in Syracuse. If I get back on the phone and tell them instead of thirty we need three hundred, this place will be crawling with Red Cross people."

This was a tough call. Would that kind of effort be justified? The Potsdam group discussed it some more. They talked with other local officials, they called NiMo, and, although it was just too early to know for sure, they decided that the situation looked serious enough to demand action. When they got back to the Red Cross rep, Mike told him no, they won't need three hundred, to which the rep sighed as if things weren't so bad after all. Instead they'd need more like six hundred, Mike told him. Whoa. Well, okay, said the rep, if they wanted them, he'd call Syracuse. Mike figured that if it turned out that they didn't need that level of support, they might look a little foolish. But if they did need it and had not gone after it, then they'd really look foolish and, more importantly, people would suffer as a result of their reluctance to act. So the call went out.

One crucial element that enabled these deliberations was

the fact that the phones were still working—working, that is, for those whose service hadn't been ripped off their houses by falling tree limbs or the weight of the ice on the line. Martha Hartle had lost her telephone, but she did have a portable two-way radio so that the rescue squad could contact her if they needed another EMT. Many others, however, still had phone service because unlike power lines, telephone lines can operate even when they fall to the ground. Marge Howe called in the early morning to tell us the obvious: she wouldn't be coming to take care of Buck today. As far as she could tell, everyone around her place was without power. She also mentioned that she might have to go sit with her daughter's father-in-law, who was dying of cancer—she had received a call indicating that the local hospice caregivers wouldn't be able to make it to his house. Dave, my neighbor across the road, had called NiMo at 3 A.M. to report that his power was out. He was told that they would send out a crew as soon as possible. That sounded hopeful. A few hours later at first light Dave had gone out to check his service drop and saw that his willow tree was laying across the wire. He called NiMo again and asked if they could send a crew out to cut the trees. This time the NiMo person said they were pretty busy.

By the time I found the radio batteries Kath had already been on the phone to work. Apparently power was out in Massena, twenty-five miles to the north, and not many people had made it in to the Alcoa plant there. Even worse, power was spotty at the plant itself. Cheap and continuous electric power was the essence of Alcoa's Massena Operations, a mammoth complex running for miles along the St. Lawrence Seaway and close to a major U.S.-Canadian hydropower dam. This proximity to hydropower was the primary reason Massena had been chosen a century ago as a site for aluminum production, despite the fact that it was located thousands of miles from the sources of alumina and the other raw materials needed to produce the metal. The smelting process demands so much power that it made economic sense to place a plant in such a location. Equally important is the need for all that power to be uninterruptible, because the process of making aluminum at the Massena smelter must not be halted. If it did go down, even for only a few hours, the structures within which the aluminum is made would be damaged, very likely beyond repair, and the cost to restart the smelter would be prohibitively high, probably in the millions of dollars. The largest employer in the state's poorest county would be crippled, if not destroyed. The economic and social ripple effects would be devastating.

While Kath discussed the situation with one of her colleagues, I powered up the portable radio so that we could find out just what was going on out there beyond our sight. I moved the dial to the Potsdam F.M. station, WPDM. Nothing but static. I slid it to the left to find North Country Public Radio. Nothing. Even worse, I didn't hear the clicks of sound you get when you cross station frequencies. I found no stations at all. The silence was disconcerting.

Off the phone, Kath debated out loud whether or not she should try to get to Massena. I told her about the radio reception. But what she wanted to know was what the roads looked like. I told her it wasn't like glass or black ice, the incredibly treacherous stuff on which you have no control. It seemed as though there was a texture to the ice. Slippery, yes, but not glare ice. In four-wheel drive she'd get some traction. It looked to me like the precipitation was oscillating occasionally between rain that turned instantly into clear ice on contact and ice crystals that gave the mixture just the tiniest bit of grit. Finally, she decided that the only essential thing she needed to do was to transmit some data to one person who she knew had gotten into the plant. If she could upload that information from her laptop through the phone lines to the Alcoa network, which so far was still up and running, she'd stay home. The question was, Did she have enough battery power in her machine to carry it off?

At 7:46 A.M. the second of two major transmission lines to the south failed, separating the north country grid from Niagara Mohawk's grid downstate. An hour later the first of three connections to Alcoa crashed. Literally. Giant NiMo towers broke apart and fell to the ground. By then Kath had succeeded in connecting and uploading to the plant and I had gone back outside to survey conditions.

The rain fell even harder. All lines sagged deeply. All roofs lay insulated beneath a creamy gray-white icing, rounding off all edges and dripping down every wall. All trees and shrubs bowed gracefully down, embedded in glass. A gently undulating sheet, pebbly white, stretched across our yards and fields from the tree line on the western horizon down to the frozen flat expanse of the Raquette River to the east.

I saw someone walking down the middle of the road toward me, his light brown coat and blue hat jumping out of the monochromatic background. I didn't recognize who it was. But just as I was about to turn to go back to the house I realized it was Dave. I don't think I had seen him in several weeks even though he lived right across the road from me. He was not smiling. Normally Dave is ebullient, quick to laugh, with an open, easy smile, but this was not a normal time. The first thing he said was that it was looking really bad. No small talk here, he got right to the matter at hand. He told me that some of his trees had landed on his roof and were lying on his electrical service. He was afraid they might take it down. If he'd had a chain saw, he'd have cut the trees down by now, he said, although pulling that off under such conditions would be pretty dangerous. I shook my head in agreement.

We speculated on the extent of the outage. Neither one of us knew anyone who had power and we were concerned that it might take the better part of the day to get ours back. That was when he told me that Lynn had picked up a generator the day before and that he and Mike had brought it down to Lynn's basement. Dave was pretty sure Lynn had gotten it fired up. "Maybe we'll go over later," I told him, "after we get the house secured." He nodded and said that he and Cindy and the kids would probably do the same.

Back inside I tried the radio again and found one station, out of Ottawa, on air. It was just talk, no music, and the talk was all about the storm and the power outages, what to do and where to go in the city. The odd thing about it was that most of the talk was speculation. The two deejays didn't really seem to know much. There were no news reports, no weather reports, just responses from callers about what they could see out of their windows. My ears perked up a few minutes into it when one of the deejays said he had just had a call from south of the border. "Someone has called us from Canton, New York, and says that the entire town is without power and is in a state of emergency." That's all he said about it. I yelled to Kath to tell her. "Wow," she said, "Ottawa, Massena, here, Canton; that's getting to be a pretty big area out of power." It could be all day before we got it back.

Mitch Teich didn't have all day. He needed to get to Canton and soon, but he had been stopped at a roadblock on his way there. When Mitch had reawakened a few hours after he lost power, he had immediately turned on his portable radio and discovered that his station, North Country Public Radio, was off air. That wasn't a total surprise, because he knew ice could play havoc with radio transmission towers. But then Mitch went up and down the dial and found nothing. This was more than just another morning of school closings, he realized. This is something much bigger, much more widespread. He'd better get to the station to see if he could help get it back on air.

It took him some time to pound enough ice off of his car so that he could get in it and see out of it. Then he had to pull across the yard and snake his way through broken trees to get out because of the downed wires on his driveway. There was just enough room between the branches to get out into the street, and it wasn't long after he left that more branches fell, leaving the yard impassable.

He made it through the deserted streets of the village and out onto the main highway, Route 11, where he met the road-block halfway between Potsdam and Canton. He was told by a man who appeared to be from a local citizens patrol that there was a travel ban, a state of emergency, and he could not continue on. Mitch started to talk his way through. "Look," he said, "I'm trying to get a radio station back on the air and that's going to make your job a lot easier." The patrolman looked at him and then waved him on to a second guy who Mitch thought looked like he was the decision maker. He told Mitch that Route 11 was blocked by fallen wires and he directed him to a side road that could get him to Canton.

The detour quickly turned into an adventure. For the first time he could see that whole trees, big trees, had come down along with power poles and tangles of wires. He was able to follow one lane through it all, but time and again he had to drive off the road and around debris to make it through. If the authorities had determined that this was the better way, he thought, then Route 11 must be a mess.

The authorities in Potsdam were by now operating in emergency mode. Despite his initial skepticism the day before, Village Police Chief McKendree fully realized now that standard procedures would be inadequate and that they had better prepare for a long siege, just in case. It was already getting chaotic at the police station with the phone ringing continually, so the chief decided to initiate an emergency work schedule. He knew his most valuable resources were his people, and burnout would be a danger over time. So the first thing he did was to split his personnel into two groups, one on the day shift—8 A.M. until 8 P.M.—and the other all night. All days off were canceled. Everyone had to come in.

The first major job that developed for the police was simply to answer calls and provide information. Initially there were lots of local calls from people wanting to know if they could get out, get supplies, get generators. Some callers seemed panicky about having enough supplies to get through the outage. And, of course, there were also the useless, annoying calls, the most common of which was "When's my cable coming back?" The correct answer, had anyone at the police station known, would have been "Not for a long time." The main signal carrier for cable T.V.—fiber optic cable—was in all variety of bad configurations: sagging, downed, broken, laying across roads, underneath trees. Nearly all of the north country's cable T.V. lines were on utility poles, and by midmorning those structures were falling at a devastating rate. Add to that the thousands of customers who lost their service drops and one could have surmised that cable television was essentially lost to the region.

As the day wore on, the police also began to get calls from people outside the region who wanted to know if they could help, if it was safe to travel into the area, if the colleges were going to begin the winter term on time, and the like. Some calls came from worried relatives who could not get through to family members in the village. The callers wanted the police to check on their families' whereabouts and safety. This concern touched upon the department's other major task: coming to the aid of village residents in need. For example, many of the morning officers worked on getting people over to the Maxcy Hall shelter, which began taking in people by 10 A.M. The very first group was a family from outside the village—no food or heat at home—who drove to Maxcy themselves. But the vast majority of those who would go there would need to be delivered.

The latter task was just one of a growing number that had to be coordinated and carried out by local officials. By midday it became clear that the Red Cross supplies from Syracuse would not be arriving anytime soon. The roads into the north country from the south were impassable. So the group at the fire station decided that Potsdam was on its own and that they'd better act accordingly. They became the central coordinating agency for the town and village. They had already declared a local state of emergency and they would later declare a water emergency, thereby restricting water use in the village. They worked on issues involving the shelter, fuel supplies, food supplies, and road maintenance, and coordinated all of their efforts with the rescue squads and police. Overall, the mode of operation at the fire and police stations was to assess a problem or need and try to line up a response by putting people and organizations together to resolve the situation. They had multiple phone lines at both locations and they were in use continually.

Calls were made periodically to Niagara Mohawk and the reports were not promising. The state of the transmission grid continued to decline. At 9:47 A.M. a segment in the east went dark, the same for a segment in the west at 12:31 P.M., as well as another major link to the Canadian grid in the north at 2:06, and lines in the southwest at 2:26.

In Massena at Alcoa, the second of three main transmission lines to the smelter went down around noon. Of the three, one brings power from the NiMo grid—that one had collapsed earlier in the morning—and two come directly from the Moses-Saunders Power Dam on the St. Lawrence. On the U.S. side the dam is run by the New York Power Authority, and is named after Robert Moses, the giant of New York construction, the man who built massive public works in New York City and numerous engineering and technological edifices across the state from the 1920s to the late 1960s. The size and scope of this particular project is daunting. Completed forty years ago, it represents to me that characteristically optimistic postwar can-do ethic of the 1950s. Harnessing nature for the good of man. If you go to the visitor's center at the dam, you learn all the impressive figures: the plant spans the length of nine football fields and houses thirty-two turbine generators, half in New York, half in Ontario. When built, the structure created a new lake—the power pool—above the dam the size of the District of Columbia. The New York side alone can produce enough power to energize a city of a million people. And the project encompasses much more than just the power dam. The entire system spans nearly forty miles along the Seaway and includes two other large dams as well as sixteen miles of dikes, all designed to restrict and redirect the flow of the great river.

Many times my family and friends have biked or jogged or boated in the vicinity of the power dam and whenever I come upon it, I'm always struck by the audacity of it all: the massive concrete structures—not nearly as dramatic as, say, the Hoover Dam, but still quite imposing—sending power out to a silver steel blizzard of towers, all hundreds of feet high, emitting a staticky buzz and heading off in rows to the horizon. This is what it takes times thousands to run our T.V.'s and VCRs and light our streets and houses, to enable others to harness nature by zapping a soup of raw materials so that we can shape it into soda cans and the skins of aircraft.

Somewhere in that forest of towers, the ice had triumphed over design, and a patrol was sent out to track down the problem. They quickly discovered that the upper section of the very first tower exiting the hydro dam had toppled over. It didn't look like that line would be repaired soon.

In the early afternoon, Niagara Mohawk crews repaired the connection to Alcoa that had gone down earlier in the morning, but the remainder of the NiMo system was in such a state that it could not supply any power to Alcoa. The safety net of having two backups to that essential one line was gone.

In contrast to the concerns of the Alcoa power engineers, many people across the region were focusing on generating just enough power to light a room or run a water pump. Judy Funston was worried about her fish. As she ventured out during the day to try to understand just what was happening, she started to think that maybe her power wouldn't be restored very soon. Her first concern was the aquarium. How long could it remain viable as the temperatures dropped and the oxygenator lay inoperable? A neighbor who had helped her out at times in the past saw her outside on the road in tears. He and his wife had a generator running at their house and once he understood what had upset Judy, he said, "Well, let's just bring the fish down here." And since they also had a spare bedroom he suggested she stay there with them. So Judy and her aquarium moved down the road.

All day long generators were being cranked up across the region. Some started right up and purred, some didn't, and many, if not most, revealed their limitations quickly. The generator outside the studios of North Country Public Radio continually overloaded and sputtered out as the workers inside tried to bring the station to air.

When Mitch finally arrived at the Canton studios, several people were already working with that generator to power up the station. They had rigged a network of extension cords from the generator in the parking lot up to the second-floor studios. For a few hours it was all trial and error. They were trying to see what they could hook up and make operational. And every time they thought they were ready to go, someone would turn on one more thing, overload the generator, and kill the power. They would then have to set up again, go back outside, restart the generator, and, most importantly, figure out what was the last thing that had been plugged in and try somehow to work around that element.

But that wasn't sufficient to get the station back on the air. Six miles away up on Waterman Hill there was no power at the transmitter. The station's chief engineer had to literally cut his way with a chain saw up the road to the transmitting tower and try to power it up with a generator. Once he had gotten that far, he then had to continually monitor the transmitter as well as refuel the generator about every hour.

Finally, by about 3 P.M. they were able to go on air. But that just raised another problem. What would they say? They had very little information, so whoever was not on air called county offices across the north country to see if they could find out just how big the emergency was. What they soon discovered was that the counties were all in the same situation. None of the officials they contacted knew the extent of the emergency other than what they could see in their locality or discover by calling others. So whoever went on air at the station had little to offer beyond "The roads are closed. Stay off the roads." After a short while they started to indicate that an emergency shelter had been set up over at the university.

But early on they really had very little air time to fill because transmission was so tenuous. Every time it went off air those listeners who had found the station would hear one of two things. If there was sudden silence, that meant the station in Canton was not transmitting. If there was sudden static, the transmitter on Waterman Hill had gone down. Both problems occurred for a variety of reasons, from merely running out of gas with one or the other generator to more serious and diffi-cult transmitter damage from the ice accumulation.

In the studio someone might be on air talking about what was known or what was being investigated and suddenly there would be a call out in the offices, "We're off the air." Instantly whoever was on the air would feel very sheepish because he or she had been talking for maybe ten minutes to no one. If the problem was at the tower, those at the station would have no idea how long it would take to get fixed. The engineer and the station had a cell phone connection but it wasn't working. In-stead, the engineer would have to drive to his house and call in and say, It's going to be X number of hours before the trans-mitter will be back on line.

Like many other people, I was an aural witness to these efforts. During the afternoon I periodically scanned the dial searching for a station. One time I happened to catch a mo-ment or two of NCPR and suddenly it was gone. Not long after that I discovered that the Potsdam F.M. station, WPDM, had also begun broadcasting intermittently. One or the other would be on for a few minutes, then gone for a long time. On the one hand, I found it unsettling that the stations were hav-ing this much difficulty, and on the other, it felt somewhat re-assuring that they were trying to make it back on the air. Late in the afternoon, I walked into Lynn and Shirley's kitchen and told them that I'd just heard WPDM and everyone there re-sponded. Really? You've been checking it? When? What did they say? Everyone wanted to know what was going on be-yond what we could see out our windows.

I was over there because I had gotten a bit antsy at home and I wanted to find out how our neighbors were doing. So I had filled a backpack with food, water, toys, and books, put Buck, all wrapped up in snowsuit and scarves, in his sled, and headed out for an adventure across the yards. Just out the door Kath and I heard something coming up the road and we watched as a van drove by slowly, the side cargo door wide open with two guys, neither of whom I recognized, carrying chain saws, sitting on the floor and dangling their legs out of the moving vehicle. Kath smiled and I said, "Well, I guess it's come to this; roving bands of chain-saw wielding . . ." I hesitated and she said, "militiamen," and I nodded quickly and added, "in a post-apocalyptic war zone" (a phrase from an episode of *The Simpsons* that I try to use whenever I can). Nothing was normal today.

Over at Lynn's we discovered a house full of people. Dave, Cindy, and their two children had come over, as had Mike and Marge and their son, who was the same age as ours. Suddenly it was a party for the kids. Shirley joked that Mike and Marge weren't sure if they wanted to be at their home, which is closer to the hospital, just in case the baby decided to come a week early, or here where it was warm. That reminded me to go check out Lynn's generator out back. On the way he told me about the previous night: they had lost power around 9 P.M. for about ten minutes, while he sat in his basement with the unit still in the box. I didn't remember losing power that early but, as I told him, I was probably dozing in a chair through it all.

When we walked out onto the back porch downstairs, we had to shout to be heard over the steady roar. "It cranked right up," he yelled to me. "Been running beautifully." The night before he had run all the wires and had everything ready to go if and when we lost power. "You called that one right," I yelled back. He nodded. "Gonna keep us out of the shelter," I said. And we both smiled as that engine hummed.

Hundreds of others around us, however, were not so fortunate. For an increasing number the shelter was looking like the only option. By the afternoon that six-hundred-bed estimate from the early morning was looking very, very low. And everything, including personnel to run the place, was in short supply. Only a few hours earlier Martha Hartle had gotten a call on her rescue-squad radio asking if she could get over to Maxcy to help out with some of the medical tasks that might arise there. Sure, she said, not having any idea what she was in for.

Although she lived close enough to walk there, even the sidewalks seemed treacherous, slippery and obstructed with branches and wires, so she was picked up by an ambulance that was out collecting people from one of the senior citizen complexes in town. Their destination, Maxcy Hall, is a large, modern, multipurpose athletic facility. In addition to a competition-level pool, it contains a large open field house on the ground floor and a smaller gym on the second. At this point the building was powered by an emergency generator that provided only some heat and some light in the main rooms of the gym and the field house. When she arrived, to her surprise, there were hundreds of people milling about upstairs and down. She could discern very few workers.

A steady influx of seniors had been arriving all afternoon as each of the village senior centers decided that their residents would be better off in the shelter. Add to that the number of seniors from private homes who were being dropped off by the police and other emergency vehicles, as well as hundreds of nonseniors, and it all looked very chaotic as Martha tried to figure out what she needed to do first. She found one registered nurse and no other medical personnel on the premises.

A few volunteers were attempting to register each person at a central area downstairs. Anyone with medical concerns had the back of his or her registration card flagged with a yellow

Post-it note. The note was supposed to list the basic information about any medical problems that the medical personnel might need to know. Martha took up the job of interviewing those who had been flagged to get a medical history and determine what, if any, medications they would need. Did they have their medications with them? When had they last taken them? When was their next medication due? In what dosage? Some of the seniors didn't know the answers to these questions. And when she'd ask each person if he or she had enough medicine to last three days, quite often the reaction was shock and fear.

The system wasn't working very well. Those entering the hall went wherever they chose. Some seniors went downstairs, some up. There was no P.A. system available so Martha found herself running upstairs and down searching for flagged people. She'd be walking through a crowd yelling, "Is Mr. Smith here? Does anyone know Mr. Smith? Are you Mr. Smith?"

Then they started to run out of registration cards and Post-it notes. They had nothing to write on. People kept arriving but the registration process had broken down. So they decided to try to organize things by moving all of the medically compromised seniors up to the second-floor gym, where it was a bit warmer than the decidedly cool field house. The only exceptions were those who required special medical equipment, like oxygen, because they didn't have facilities upstairs like oxygen tanks and ventilators.

So Martha and some others began to approach every senior downstairs who gave some indication of a medical condition and ask each to gather his or her belongings and move upstairs. For many of the seniors this was a traumatic environment. Some were confused and scared, some quite frail, some sick. Some had difficulty merely walking, much less gathering up their belongings and carrying them all the way up to the second floor. But somehow with help they did it. All of the designated seniors moved up to the gym, all of the others moved down. Now, thought Martha, she could finally gather the crucial information needed to keep these people safe and healthy for the short term.

Then, just as she was beginning her rounds, the gym went black and stayed black. No power. Suddenly the word came from downstairs: herd everybody back down the stairs to the field house. Many of these people refused to leave their belongings. They were afraid they'd never find them again. Martha was extremely nervous. She was sure that at any moment one of them was going to fall, have a heart attack, a stroke, drop dead, something terrible. But they all made it down. And, of course, once they were all down, the power came back on upstairs. Again, she was told to try to get the seniors back up there. By that time, however, some SUNY students who had returned to campus a week early to prepare for the upcoming semester had arrived and were recruited to carry all of the clothes and bags back up, as well as assist anyone who needed help climbing stairs.

But Martha was not happy and she told one of the other volunteers, "I'm not moving these people again. There is just no way that they can be moved. If the power goes out we'll work through it." She said this as if she had made that decision but didn't know who was in charge or whom she should report to. Then a question came up about one patient that she didn't know the answer to, so she said she'd go find out. While discussing the issue downstairs in the command office, she asked who was in charge of the medical facility and the answer was simple: "You," she was told. "You're in charge."

In the course of the afternoon, Martha had gone from a part-time EMT to the head of the medical wing of a disaster relief shelter housing far more people than expected. Already the population was well over a thousand and continually growing.

Back upstairs she continued with the other volunteers to try to organize things and help people out, constantly going from one patient to another, helping some to the bathroom—in the dark with flashlights—getting others drinks, answering questions, helping with medications, offering reassuring words. Many of these people were very nervous and Martha realized that it was important to try to give them some emotional support in whatever way possible.

It was a struggle but the volunteers were trying to provide reasonable living conditions for everyone. That evening food was trucked in from the Massena school district twenty-five miles away. Apparently, the school's food service had the wherewithal to make and distribute food. But as night came on it was clear there would be too few beds available. Some of the seniors would have nothing more than a chair, a blanket, and a little dog mat.

And the rain continued to fall. Around 6 P.M. the Alcoa smelter lost power when automatic relays at the power dam shut down. The Power Authority system was beginning to collapse because it was no longer connected to the northeastern power grid and no longer had a steady demand on its power. As a result, the system became unstable. Knowing that time was critical, Power Authority technicians attempted again and again to restore power and finally, after about seventy minutes, they succeeded and the Alcoa technicians were able to restart the smelting process. Throughout the evening, however, the unstable system caused numerous power fluctuations that played havoc with a variety of devices in the smelter.

At 6:31 P.M. the only remaining energized section on the western side of the NiMo grid went dark, and shortly thereafter everything that had remained powered in the east failed.

The grid was now dead. All connections to all sources of power, save Moses-Saunders to Alcoa, were lost.

All across the region people found themselves facing the spreading darkness under unfamiliar circumstances. Where Judy Funston was staying, the generator had been shut down to give it a rest. When Judy could no longer see well enough to do needlework or read, she found herself at a loss, not ready for sleep but unable to do anything else but lie in the darkness. Across the road from me, Dave had cooked supper outside on a Coleman stove and then, as the house got colder and colder, decided he'd better do something to keep the pipes from freezing. He turned off the water, drained all the lines, drained the hot water tank, and put a bit of windshield wiper fluid in all the traps under the sinks. At nightfall he and Cindy and their children all huddled together in the same bed.

Three miles away in the village of Hannawa Falls, Buck's sitter, Marge Howe, thought she was settling down to sleep as she curled up on a cramped little couch in the home of her daughter's dying father-in-law, Hubie. This was typical of Marge. She's been taking care of people for most of her sixty-seven years. She raised five of her own but she's also commonly referred to as the woman who has raised half of Potsdam. For most of her adult life she has worked as a daycare provider for dozens and dozens of families in the area. And many of her "kids" now have children of their own.

Marge had known Hubie for thirty years and was well aware that since September he'd been deteriorating. By then his cancer had progressed so that he could no longer drive and he became increasingly homebound. Thirteen years before his wife had died of cancer, and now Hubie was facing the same fate.

At Christmastime, when his son and Marge's daughter drove up from their home in North Syracuse to visit, they had asked Marge if she could stay with him at times when neither they nor his nurses could be there. So Marge went over several times between Christmas and New Year's. A week later, with the power out, she suspected that he'd be needing help again.

In the late afternoon the Hannawa Falls Fire Department had picked Marge up and driven her the mile to Hubie's house through the tangled mess that the main road had become, weaving on one lane around downed trees and wires. When she had arrived, she had learned that the house was being heated by a wood-burning stove in one room and a fireplace in the room where Hubie stayed. Usually he'd wear his oxygen mask but periodically he'd take it off, turn off the oxygen and smoke his cigarettes and drink his Pepsis, two habits that he would never give up.

Marge had also discovered that the hospice had dropped off a large oxygen tank designed to last for several days; but, unfortunately, it required electricity to run. His portable tanks— he had one going and one spare—operated without power. In addition, arrangements had been made to have another patient live at the house to help Hubie when he could, a man recovering from triple bypass surgery. He stayed in the adjacent room with the woodstove.

Marge tended to Hubie during the early evening, cooking soup on the stove, helping him eat, helping him to and from the bathroom, keeping both fires and an oil lamp going. She also had help again from the fire department. One of the firefighters, a woman named Janet Brown, came over to hook up the second portable tank for Hubie. But after she left, Hubie discovered that the new tank was only partially filled. He thought, though, that it should last until morning. So around 7 P.M. Marge told Hubie that it was time to get him settled in for the night. She helped him into his hospital bed and she laid down on the small love seat nearby.

Around the time Marge was preparing Hubie's supper, I was discovering a local A.M. station out of Massena that was providing continual storm information—mostly firsthand reports from callers. As I cooked over the open flame of our camp stove, which sat inside a large iron skillet perched upon our now defunct electric range top, a man came on the air who had just been driving through the county. "Up in Potsdam," he said, "it's bad. They're getting hit real bad up there." I nodded to myself. No way we're getting power back tonight.

Darkness fell and the station began to fade as local A.M. stations do after sunset. But I was able to listen long enough to hear Sandy, the host, play a single advertisement several times, the only ad he was running. It was for a car dealership, and the first time I heard it Sandy made a comment like, Well, we have to pay our bills here so I'm going to run this spot.

It sounded so utterly out of place, almost jarring. Under any other circumstance, of course, I wouldn't have even noticed it or the thousand others I may have seen and heard on a given day, but now the context had been altered. It was like all the times I've played television ads for students in my mass media courses. Invariably, when students see ads in the classroom, they laugh at how ridiculous they appear or they cringe at the ads' stupidity and ineptitude. But the ads are not inept no matter how ridiculous they seem. Those ads are quite powerful, but they lose their power when shown out of their natural environment, that amorphous media soup we swim through every day, all day. On this night, somehow that environment had been ruptured, and, for the moment at least, there seemed to be no place for advertisements.

Nonetheless, the ice storm would have commercial appeal, and although it hadn't yet received detailed coverage in the United States, it was already a big story in Canada. While no one in the north country saw it, at 10 P.M. the storm was the only story featured on CBC's *The National,* Canada's nationally broadcast nightly news show, hosted by Peter Mansbridge.

The opening set the dramatic tone: "Tonight: another special edition of *The National.* Iced in, from Ottawa to the Maritimes—how people are coping with the cold. And why this may be the storm of the century." Then, after the opening banners, "Good evening from Montreal," said Mansbridge. "Once again tonight, a city at the heart of a crisis in the cold; a crisis that has up to three million people anxiously wondering when will the freezing rain stop, and when will the power start? As so many people feared, the emergency here has deepened. Hydro crews waged a losing battle last night; a battle against another wave of a punishing storm. And it's not over yet."

About ten segments followed, starting with an overview of the storm's impact. A weather map revealed the breadth of the storm. "As you can see, it cuts a huge swath, bringing misery from Mississippi to the Maritimes." What had caused flooding in North Carolina and Tennessee now brought disaster to the northeast. Mansbridge went on to describe the conditions: states of emergency throughout the afflicted areas, the military mobilized, a million without power in Montreal alone, two hundred thousand in Vermont and Maine (no mention of New York), and at least six deaths. This latter item served as the lead to a segment entitled "Ice Tragedies" that went on to describe the influx of people to shelters across the region. Other segments reported on the storm's connection to El Niño, the state of the storm in different communities, the responses of both federal and provincial governments, the dangers facing the utility workers as they worked long hours in difficult conditions, and the fears and struggles of people trying to cope.

The latter stories were of the type that seemed to say that our true natures are revealed in times of crisis. At one point, for example, reporter Mark Kelley described how there had been a tremendous sense of solidarity among people who were trying to help one another. But then he quickly added that the sense of community may have been fraying under the strain. To which Peter Mansbridge added, "You know we also saw today the first signs of starting to point the finger of blame, and you get this at times like this in these crises, and it usually comes around day three like this one is, where people are starting to look for something beyond the weather to lay blame."

Already, the behavior of "victims" was falling into familiar patterns. The shaping of experience had begun. But the question of just what was our true nature was left hanging, just as viewers are left hanging before each commercial break. The transcript of the broadcast reads:

> **MANSBRIDGE** And later, on the *Magazine* with Hana Gartner:
>
> **HANA GARTNER** Twenty-four hours in a city without lights; what to do when modern life shuts down. For some, it's the adventure of a lifetime. For others, a recipe for disaster. Living through a crisis. The Long, Dark Night.
>
> (COMMERCIAL BREAK)

And later,

> **GARTNER** We're going to take a short break right now. When we come back, overnight in a city without lights. And a cry in the dark . . . And a voice of calm . . . Montreal's 911 centre, the "Eye of the Storm," when the *National* continues.
>
> (COMMERCIAL BREAK)[1]

Disasters are full of good hooks to keep us watching, and it is just these kinds of stories that shape the way we make sense of our so-called direct experience. While on any given day most of what we learn is mediated in some way or another, on this day for everyone in the storm very little was. We had to make sense of these random and indeterminate events on our own and that is exhausting. Earlier in the day, many people searched and searched for a radio station, ostensibly to find out crucial information but, I suspect, also because we sought the comfort of having someone else tell us how to interpret events. I don't doubt that if somehow the power had suddenly returned that night, I would have been riveted to the words of the CBC correspondents as they characterized my experience for me.

But the power didn't come on and *The National* played for other people in other places. And as it did, many of us slept. But not Marge. Just as she would doze off, Hubie would wake her with one thing or another. "Marge. Put wood on the fire," or a little while later, "Marge. Marge. Gotta go to the bathroom." After several of these, he finally seemed to settle down and she tried again to fall asleep.

Sometime past midnight all was quiet when suddenly she heard Hubie again. He called her name several times.

"What is it, Hubie?"

"I haven't got any oxygen."

"But Hubie," she said, "we just hooked that one up."

"I haven't got any oxygen!" He pointed to the gauge. "Look, it's low."

Marge got up with the flashlight and checked it. She thought the man staying in the other room might know what to do, so she called out to him, waking him up.

"What the hell do you want?!" he yelled.

"Hubie's low on oxygen."

"What am I supposed to do about it?"

"Well," said Marge, "I don't know what to do either." Realizing that Hubie's "helper" was not going to be helping, she got over to the phone and called the local hospital. Hubie's breathing got shorter and quicker. He's getting upset, she realized. When she got the emergency room she quickly explained the situation.

"Can you deliver some oxygen?" she asked, not realizing the incredible strain all emergency services were working under. The hospital was maxing out on its capabilities. Resources had to be directed on a priority basis.

"No, I'm sorry, you are going to have to bring him in."

"I can't bring him in now."

"Well, we aren't able to get an ambulance out there right now."

Marge needed to figure out how to get him there. She said she'd get back to them. Then she decided to try the number of the hospice woman she had dealt with in the past. After a number of rings, the woman answered. Marge repeated the story and the woman asked how much oxygen was left in the tank. Marge told her.

"Alright," she said, "that should last him a little while. I'll call you back."

Hubie was panicking, wheezing, sucking down the oxygen at an increased rate. No power, no generator to get at all that oxygen sitting in the big tank. Marge sat in the dark listening to Hubie's rasp and waiting for the phone to ring.

origins of a grid, part 2

saturday, october 4, 1941

Sleep came easily to the old man. Maybe it was the muffled, sputtering rhythm of the powerboat up ahead, maybe the un-expected warmth of the autumn sun. Whatever it was, on a bright fall afternoon while he was floating across the St. Lawrence River in his rowboat, sleep came again to Tom Vallance. Not that he didn't have reason to be tired. He had rowed his boat, a sixteen-footer he'd built himself, from his farm on Croil's Island all the way to Massena to buy groceries. Although he made this trip every week, rowing downriver and back up was rigorous work, even for an old dairy farmer like himself.

But on this day, the routine had changed. While he was preparing to row back home loaded down with supplies, a man in a motorboat pulled near and offered him a tow. Tom accepted and tossed over his bowline. Then he settled back against his cargo and closed his eyes to the afternoon sun. The little flotilla puttered along.

For most people who spent their time there, river life was quiet. Farmers tended to their herds and tilled their fields along the meandering shady shores or across the large islands. Fishermen searched for black bass in the pools upriver from the many patches of swift whitewater. For those who knew those spots and how to approach them, the river could be bountiful. On a given morning a skilled angler might pull thirty or forty black bass out of one of those pools. And that was not all. Coursing through those waters were a myriad of creatures, from little sunnies and larger pike to the ancient sturgeon, a giant among freshwater fish. Photos of these monsters were often circulated among river people, photos of local men, tall men, standing next to a catch that matched their height head to tail, a fish trussed up like deer.[1]

The water was clean—if you got thirsty on your boat, you dipped a cup in the river and drank from it—and swift; the shoreline was variegated with tree-lined coves and jutting points; the river was full of fish. From Ogdensburg to Massena, most of the St. Lawrence was still a wild, beautiful river. But other segments didn't seem so unspoiled. For centuries, the river had been the object of ambitious undertakings. Thousands of workers with their increasingly sophisticated tools had dug canals and built locks, diverted strategic flows and dammed swift currents, all with the intent of overcoming the impediments caused by the river's descent from its height in the Great Lakes down to its mouth in the North Atlantic. The goal was to transform the powerful outlet of the lakes into a docile vessel of commerce.

In many ways the river served as a measuring rod to gauge man's will to control nature, because even in Tom Vallance's day its most difficult passage lay largely untouched. That passage, the most intractable stretch of the entire river, churned off the port side of Tom's boat as he lay sleeping, oblivious to the approaching roar.

Depending on your perspective, where Tom lived and worked was either a vast, breathtaking maze of islands, trees, rocks, rapids, and pools, or a major bottleneck in a two-thousand-mile highway. From the east an oceangoing vessel could travel the St. Lawrence a thousand miles from the Atlantic Ocean through the Gulf of St. Lawrence and up the river to Montreal. From the west a Great Lakes vessel could travel from Duluth, Minnesota, on Lake Superior 1,200 miles to Ogdensburg with only one tight squeeze in the Welland Canal that connected Lake Erie and Lake Ontario. But the 120 miles of river between Ogdensburg and Montreal posed serious impediments to large boat traffic. In particular, the fifty-mile span from Ogdensburg past Louisville to St. Regis, the old Haudenosaunee village, was laced with four stretches of rapids that blocked the passage of large ships.[2] One of those four rapids was known as the Long Sault, probably the most dangerous length of the entire river. And for Tom, that is where the changing sound pierced his sleep.

He awoke not to the rhythmic engine but to the ever-increasing roar of rushing water. Somehow his bowline had cut loose from the motorboat and now his own craft was picking up speed, heading not to the island and home but directly toward the crashing waters of the Long Sault Rapids. By the time he got his oars in the water, the boat was cresting the northern headwall, the most violent part of the run, and he couldn't stop it. Everything blurred; a sixty-seven-year-old man shooting the rapids backward, flailing the oars desperately, trying to gain some control over water, rocks, and gravity, hoping to God he wouldn't get tossed into the boil.

Life could be harsh in the world in which Tom Vallance and his river neighbors lived. It was difficult and isolated in many ways. It was also connected to vast enterprises under the watchful eyes of powerful men, men who knew the importance of the river in global terms but who knew nothing of life on it. Croil's Island, where Tom farmed, sat across from Louisville Landing, which from the time of its earliest settlers—people like Powell, his companions, their neighbors and survivors—had grown steadily into a lively and important hub of river life. The landing may have been quite close to the big rapids that constricted continental commerce, but its strategic location, a point with an advantageous crossing to the islands and Canada, enabled a small but vibrant local economy.

A few years before Powell began clearing his farm, a land developer and lumberman named John Gibson had built at the landing a custom house where trade between the countries could be processed and duties collected. Constructed out of two-foot-wide pine planks, with tree limbs for rafters, the building would serve for a hundred years as the easternmost point of entry along the St. Lawrence into the United States. In the first few decades of the nineteenth century, a hotel, a general store, and a post office were built nearby. Organized religion became established in the 1820s with the arrival of Methodist preachers. And in the 1850s, about the time Franklin Hough was writing the first history of the region, local worshippers built a community church, which for years served as a Methodist house of worship but eventually became a Congregationalist center that could hold a variety of Christian services. The adjacent graveyard was the burial site for many of the original settlers.

In those early days crossings between the landing and the Canadian community of Aultsville on the north side were made on rowboats, which later gave way to a horse-powered ferry. With a side wheel like the well-known Mississippi paddle wheels, the forty-five-foot scow was powered by two horses on a running tread. Horse power eventually gave way to steam, and for several years two steam-powered ferries carried people and goods between the nations. Over time these ferries came to serve as the main means of connection among communities on both sides of the river from Ogdensburg to

Massena, and they provided the infrastructure for most of the economic activity.

Louisville Landing became a primary port of trade in horses, cattle, sheep, and poultry. In addition, its location just above the big rapids made the landing a strategic way station in the nation's huge logging industry. Cut logs from the vast midwestern forests of Wisconsin were floated through the Great Lakes and down the St. Lawrence. When they reached Louisville, the massive flotillas had to be tied up above the landing and then drams—small sections of logs—were pulled off and taken down through the Long Sault by twenty-man teams of expert river drivers.[3]

In addition to its role as a trading center, the landing also became a popular stopping point for tourists and a party spot for locals. A half-dozen miles inland were the mineral baths at Massena Springs, an extremely popular destination by the turn of the century. Tourists would disembark their river crafts at the landing, stay the night there at the hotel, and take a stage the next day to the springs.[4] By the late 1920s a popular dance hall was operating on a tiny island just off the landing. During Prohibition, Mino's Dance Hall drew people from across the region for a couple of reasons. First of all, it featured some wonderful acts that one could often see in the north country. Big bands shook the crude stage in the rickety pavilion. One summer night, for example, Cab Calloway and his orchestra had Mino's jumping. But there was also another unique feature if one was interested. In the late afternoon before a show, cars riding low on their shocks as if loaded down with freight would come across on the ferry from the north side. Drivers would pull off onto the dirt track that ran along the shore and drop burlap bags in the reeds and rushes along the river. Later on, local kids would be paid a penny for every beer bottle they could retrieve from the river and bring to a man selling Canadian beer to thirsty dancers at the inflated price of a dollar a bottle. In the great tradition of General Brown and the potash smugglers of a century before, this stretch of river was a place of entrepreneurial possibilities, legal and illegal.

But for Tom Vallance on that day it was a place of blind terror. Later he would remember nothing of the ride. Somehow his boat stayed intact and he stayed in it as he scraped and crashed his way through the worst of the rapids faster than he'd ever gone on that river before. Just as he came abreast of another big island, Barnhart Island, his boat finally overturned and Tom thrashed about trying to swim to shore. As he got closer he was able to call out for help and a man across the way on Sheek Island heard him. Quickly, the rescuer and a companion rowed over and helped pull Tom ashore. A few days later he was informed that he was only the "third known man in history to shoot the tumultuous Long Sault Rapids in a light craft."[5]

From any distance Tom may have looked like a lost figure bounding down the fall line of a remote and lonely stretch of violent water. But it was just this strip of river in those very years before America's entry into the war that was the focus of much debate among President Franklin Roosevelt, Canadian Prime Minister Mackenzie King, governors, premiers, congressmen, members of parliament, military leaders, and engineers. Around the time Tom Vallance awoke on the precipice, the power elites in Washington and Ottawa were trying to figure out how to bridge those rapids once and for all.

Others had tried in the past, but with severely limited scopes. Technical developments in shipping continually outpaced the development of the river. In 1834, twenty-eight years after Abner Powell and his three American neighbors plunged to their deaths in the icy river just above the Long

Sault Rapids, Canadians began to dig a trench on the northern side to enable safe passage around them. The first canal was nine feet wide. By the turn of the century it had been expanded to a size large enough to carry a 250-foot boat with a fourteen-foot draft, a big boat by many standards. But in 1940 this canal was nowhere near big enough to handle the lakers or the oceangoing ships that would make passage truly profitable, or to carry the thousands of new naval ships needed to fight the coming war in Europe.

By the fall of 1940, it seemed clear to decision makers in both capitals that transforming the river into what they called the Seaway could help the war effort in two ways: first, the Great Lakes could become a strategic and protected shipbuilding machine to support the naval war; second, the falling river in the "International Rapids" section, that stretch from Ogdensburg to St. Regis, could become a major source of hydropower. Although there was already a St. Lawrence powerhouse providing electricity to the Alcoa plant in Massena, a massive increase in the amount of electricity was needed to fire more aluminum potlines to supply defense contractors with that essential element for the growing war machine.

On October 16, 1940, President Roosevelt, by executive order, established the St. Lawrence Advisory Committee and charged it with the task of initiating this project. The president allocated the committee an operating budget of $1 million. Several months later the governor of New York, Herbert Lehman, followed Roosevelt's lead by proposing to increase the funding for the New York Power Authority, which, like Roosevelt's federal committee, was also charged with developing power on the St. Lawrence.[6] But one year after that, when the governor's new budget director—J. Buckley Bryan, my wife's grandfather and the source of our son's name—revealed the 1942 state budget, there was no push to develop St.

Lawrence power.[7] The war demanded too many resources and too much political capital, and the project failed to get beyond the design stage.

Eventually, of course, this condition changed. A decade later America was undergoing a cultural and economic transformation of unprecedented proportions: from war to recovery, from shortages of essentials to the promise of commercial plenty, from a culture of sacrifice to the beginnings of a culture of consumption, from a time of extreme pain and destruction to an age of progress, from radio to television. In this new world, we would learn, technological development was the engine of freedom.

In a 1952 film celebrating the sesquicentennial of Massena —a film professionally produced in the tradition of those classic midcentury newsreels—the unfailingly eager narrator speaks with a radio announcer's crisp, deep, good-natured voice, loping along over the tinny and earnestly upbeat music. After recounting a few highlights of the town's 150 years (the river, the logging, the farming, the aluminum), he tells us about this bright new world we live in. And it's all about consuming new goods. Over pastel images of shiny cars with gorgeous tailfins, streamlined two-toned buses, and pert, well-dressed pedestrians bustling about the downtown streets, we hear that yes, it's a much different town today: "Massenans of even fifty years ago would be amazed at the difference! Today Massena has a shopping center complete with all the conveniences of modern living. There are well-stocked department stores, drugstores, restaurants, theaters, banks and business places, filling stations and garages, everything in fact that people need for easy, comfortable living." As we see a man pushing a power mower across his lawn, we are told that "today all our citizens enjoy a way of life their ancestors never even dreamed of."

Then suddenly the images change from a celebration of

Anytown USA to something far more specific. We see two men standing in front of a microphone in the darkness, lit only by a flashlight. One man rings a bell and announces the start of a town meeting. The other, holding the flashlight, reads from a sheet of paper. It's supposed to be the start of the national radio broadcast of *America's Town Meeting of the Air,* tonight live from Massena's sesquicentennial celebration, but there's no electricity in the town. We learn that a severe storm had hit the north country only two hours before, uprooting trees, destroying homes and cars, and knocking out power. Two days later, the anniversary's large "historical society luncheon" would become the first hot meal since the storm for residents, a combination celebration dinner and shelter meal all at once.

The film transforms into a disaster story as the camera pans ruined houses and flooded streets. The music changes to the kind of ominous tones that might have backed newsreels of bombed-out cities of Europe a decade earlier. The man with the flashlight says that emergency measures have been taken to relay the broadcast through a telephone line to the American Broadcasting Company's nationwide network. "It is fitting," he continues, "that the celebration of this 150th anniversary of Massena and the 50th anniversary of Alcoa's plant here should be opened by . . ." I want to say, "a power outage," but he says, "such a distinguished program as *Town Meeting of the Air.*" No matter. To put it in the current vernacular, it's all about the power.

Eventually the film recovers that fifties can-do attitude, and Massena again becomes Small Town America Moving into the Future with High Hopes. Nearly fifty years later this jumble of scenes is telling: that fledgling vision of the new nation was built upon the foundation of reliable electric power, and (cue the soundtrack: industriously eager music rising) to make it work we needed more of it, a lot more.

june 16, 1956

As he stood before the distinguished members of the Canadian Club of Ottawa on this early summer day in the middle of the great Seaway construction project, Robert Moses made it clear that he and his compatriots were men of action not of words, builders not manipulators; they dealt with substance not image and would follow a clear path and avoid the diversions of politics:

> We do not build by metaphors. I suppose that on the St. Lawrence the simplest conception to grasp is that of a great river as a moving road which we are attempting to block and bypass. Our obstacles are not merely physical. They are human in the sense that we must move people and change established uses. They include, unfortunately, obscure laws, unusually complex, overlapping administrative agencies, conflicting personalities, private selfishness, and the stilted terminology of diplomatic usage. Builders get gray hair not from the accidents and hazards of construction, but from the maddening opposition of those who seemingly have little interest in the direct route to a goal.

Yes, Moses was known to drive projects swiftly to their completion, but he was, of course, a skilled manipulator. As Robert Caro showed in his famous and exhaustive portrait of the man, *The Power Broker,* Moses argued from a particularly powerful position; he argued that he was interested not in politics but in the public good.[8] By creating an image as a protector of the public's interest, Moses built an unassailable bulwark of power. And the Seaway, everyone seemed to agree, was clearly a public good.

We must subdue the rapids so that the St. Lawrence may again run unimpeded to the sea. We must restore and enhance the scenery of the river and provide for recreation for masses of visitors. We must insure a seaway navigable by large ships which will bring the ports of the Great Lakes to the Atlantic and give our two countries a new seacoast of 7,000 miles. We must force a mighty stream into the penstocks which turn the turbines of a burgeoning industrial empire unimagined by Cartier and Champlain. We must bridge the gap between the ages of steam and atomic energy. We must find or invent some giant Bunyan with a blowtorch to melt Arctic ice. In this task, however stupendous, all those in any way responsible should rise above human pettiness and frailties to something approaching statesmanship.[9]

By controlling the river we will free it. By cutting into it and changing its course we will make it more beautiful for more people than ever before. By channeling its flow in just this one region we will create a vast new geography. By doing all this, we will span Fulton's nineteenth century and Three Mile Island's twentieth. Before our grand undertaking, falling water was an impediment; now it will be the fuel of unprecedented progress.

And while this protector of the public good, this mighty colossus who would bend nature to our ambitious design, was intoning those words, his operatives were manipulating the powerless to achieve this goal. Suddenly, quietly, people along the south shore of the river started to see men walking across their property, taking notes and leaving without saying a word, trespassers to some, a curiosity to others. Later, these people

would receive letters instructing them to come to an office—
the old hotel at Louisville Landing—to sign an agreement on
the worth of their properties. For the greater good, the land
buyers were working to dispossess the local landowners of the
river.

To build the Seaway and its giant power dam, the New
York Power Authority needed to claim miles of shoreline and
thousands of acres. People had to move. And from the start, as
Robert Moses made clear, those who acquiesced were serving
the public interest; those who objected were self-aggrandizing
opportunists. In a Power Authority brochure designed to explain the process of acquiring the necessary land, Moses spoke
directly to those who stood in the way of progress:

> They must make some sacrifices for the common
> good. It is our responsibility and wish to make these
> sacrifices as small as possible. . . .
>
> There is, however, a sharp line of distinction be-
> tween the interests of those who face the loss of their
> homes and must, therefore, be uprooted and settled
> elsewhere and those whose main concern is specula-
> tion on increases in land values which may be brought
> about by the power and seaway projects. The specula-
> tor has been the loudest complainant up until the
> present time and not the resident on whom the great-
> est hardship falls. . . .
>
> We cannot in this matter be swayed by personal
> feelings or yield to the many pressures exerted by
> those who are more concerned with protecting pres-
> ent interests than in the future of a great public under-
> taking. We recognize the human side of this problem
> but we do not propose to be cajoled, threatened, in-

timidated or pressured into modifying sound engineering plans to suit selfish private interests.[10]

In contrast, many along the river felt as though they were
being cajoled, threatened, intimidated, and pressured into giving up their lands. In Canada, public protest against the land
grab grew so loud that it actually reached key decision makers
in Ottawa, resulting in a much-publicized effort to improve
the compensation of the dispossessed and relocate entire towns
to the satisfaction of most of the affected population. But in
other jurisdictions, there was much unhappiness. Mohawk
lands deeded to the tribe in perpetuity by past treaties on both
sides of the border were simply canceled and renegotiated so
that the project could gain the segments needed. And the concerns of landowners in New York were largely ignored.

First of all, some locals claimed that the land buyers were
following a strategy designed to depress the value of all properties. While Robert Moses said that the goal should be to make
the "sacrifices as small as possible," those living along the
southern shore felt as though the goal was to make their *compensation* as small as possible. This would be achieved in two
ways: one, landowners were offered what was called "market
value" for their property. The problem with this was that the
market value had been depressed since 1940, when it looked as
though the Seaway project might go through to aid the war effort. Two, that value was manipulated downward through
some skillful strategies. For example, in a given area a land
buyer might start the negotiations by approaching the poorest
inhabitants first in order to set a low baseline. By offering a
small amount to those who had the least and who might jump
at anything, the land buyer could then go to a neighbor and
say, This (deflated) price is what we're paying your neighbor,

here is your (deflated) price. This strategy pitted neighbor against neighbor, splitting family from family and beginning the process of breaking the community apart. The achievements of the earliest settlers of these shores—the pioneers who had carved out connections among their families as protection against the forces that would destroy them—were undone by the land buyers.

Overall, the land buyers made it clear that if the locals didn't accept the first offer, the second would be lower. The longer you wait, the argument went, the less you will get. This reasoning violated standard market forces that say a desired property increases in value the more crucial it becomes to those who need it, but this wasn't a free market. State law had been tested and upheld that would enable the Power Authority to take lands with little or no compensation if, in the end, it had to do so to complete its work. So the message was, The first offer is the best; take it and run.

Most did, but with great reluctance. A 1954 newspaper article focused on the town of Louisville to get a glimpse of the impending losses: several thousand acres, sixty farms, several hundred cottages, a third of the entire taxable land of the town. Families who had lived on the river for over a hundred years would have to move away: Martinus Casselman, whose great-great-grandfather cleared virgin forest to make his home; the direct descendents of Joseph Bradford, one of the original settlers, who walked there all the way from Vermont to look over the land before buying it; the Stone farm, where 145 years before the Stone family's ancestors had cleared the land and built the house that the descendents still occupied—all had to move. The Casaw farm, by Louisville Landing, had eighty-four acres and twenty head of cattle. Mr. Casaw wanted to keep farming, the article says, but he had discovered that the price of farmland elsewhere was "out of sight." Said another farmer, one whose entire island spread would be lost, "See if you can replace this view." [11]

While some publications covered the displacement story, the overwhelming majority of media coverage was focused on the gargantuan construction project. In the one history of the project that did discuss the plight of the dispossessed, Carleton Mabee pointed out—albeit in a footnote—that the size of the project had been carefully monitored and communicated while the human costs had not. "It is ironic," wrote Mabee, "that while the Seaway agencies kept precise records of how much steel and concrete went into the Seaway, they did not keep precise records of the number of persons the Seaway forced out of the way." [12] But even when the topic of moving people was presented, the most common story—one that made national and international news at the time—was the amazing house-moving technology employed during the project. Pictures of houses intact on top of giant motorized platforms inching their way down roads made many newspapers. The accompanying stories usually emphasized that the ride would be so smooth that the owners wouldn't have to wrap a dish or take a picture off the wall. Mabee recounted a live national television broadcast from the Canadian side in which a family is at home finishing breakfast and twenty minutes later movers lift the house off its foundation and begin the mile trek to a new location. Forty minutes later the house has been lowered onto its new site, with power, water, sewage, and telephone all reconnected. And before the sign-off, "as millions of people saw on TV, tea had been served from the kitchen." [13]

When I look at the histories and written accounts of that time, it seems clear that the objections of the locals, especially in New York, were utterly dwarfed by the size and drama of the project. Most accounts mentioned that people along the river had lost their homes, businesses, cottages, farms, schools, and churches, but those accounts all seemed to follow one of two paths. Either they spoke almost entirely about the efforts by the Canadian government to build new towns for their dispossessed and, at best, offered just a passing reference to the plight of the New Yorkers and Mohawks. Or the accounts mentioned briefly the hardships but quickly pointed out that in the end, even the dispossessed were happy to see the grand achievement of the Seaway finally realized.

In his exhaustive history of the river from Cartier to the Seaway, William Willoughby discussed opposition to the Seaway from shippers, bankers, railroads, coal miners, private power utilities, governments, and other commercial interests but ignored the opposition of the river people.[14] Lowell Thomas, in his history, discussed the Canadian relocation effort at some length and noted only that relocations on the southern shore were fewer in number than on the northern shore. He did not discuss the changing look of the river in terms of its natural beauty but pointed out that "the Seaway and Power scheme is a matter of modern progress and international prosperity, and no one who believes in progress and prosperity would deny that the correct decision was made."[15] A major article in a 1959 issue of *National Geographic* discussed only the Canadian dispossession and quoted only one person, an eighty-seven-year-old Canadian woman who had had to move. "It really hasn't been bad, being moved," she was quoted as saying. "You can't expect the world to stop changing just because you're getting old."[16] Similar sentiments served as the primary message of Clara Judson's *St. Lawrence Seaway*,[17] while John Brior's *Taming of the Sault* noted that after the people had been moved, the quality of nature was improved by the work of the engineers: "With the completion of the World's 8th Wonder, the scars left by man and machine have been healed. The dis-

rupted countrysides in northern New York and southern Ontario bloom again in natural beauty with the artistic hand of the
planners leaving the area more attractive than before." [18]

Even Carleton Mabee's history, which devoted an entire
chapter to the issue and described in quite moving prose the
losses of the river people, was devoted primarily to the Canadian relocation and concluded that in the end most of the dispossessed were satisfied with their treatment.

A lone but powerful counterview to such acceptance
came nearly thirty years after the Seaway was completed from
a historian examining the project's impact on the Haudenosaunee. Laurence Hauptman in his history of Native
American activism after World War II pointed out that not
only did the Seaway project dispossess the Haudenosaunee of
land but it led to the pollution of remaining lands, ruining
much of their fishing and farming. These events, argued
Hauptman, triggered the rise of the militant Red Power
movement. [19]

I found my way to these histories when I began to investigate the construction of the regional power grid, which led
me, of course, to the Moses-Saunders Power Dam and the Seaway. When I searched Caro's massive study of Robert Moses, I
discovered very little about the Seaway project. Over his lifetime Moses's impact was vast, and the Seaway was just one
more project in a half-decade's productivity. But there was
one passage that stood out and urged me to follow this path
further.

Caro recounted a story told him by a former aide to Averell Harriman, who was New York's governor during the construction of the Seaway. In attempting to describe the balance
of power between Moses and the governor, the aide remembered that Harriman " 'said he was getting reports from the
local people up on the St. Lawrence that Moses was going to

tear out lots of the homes of little people along the St. Lawrence for his parkways [the public recreation areas that accompanied the Seaway development], and the little people need to be protected.' " The aide and a companion traveled to the river and found out that, yes, this was true. " 'There were cottages lining the shore near Massena . . . nice looking cottages, too, not luxurious but nice, cottages into which you could tell loving care had gone. Moses was obliterating them.' " Somehow, word of this little investigation made its way to Moses and he confronted Harriman. The governor's men, Moses made clear, were talking to people they shouldn't be talking to. " 'And that was the last we heard of the little people,' continued the aide. 'It was never brought up again.' " Shortly thereafter, noted Caro, Harriman announced that he was naming the power dam after Moses.[20]

While this story provides some insight into the balance of power between the people on the river and those deciding their fates, the more important issue was why the governor backed down and enabled Moses's public to triumph over another public. Why did that amorphous public who wanted parks win over the public who owned land? This type of tension between public and private still fuels controversies around the nation: in the nearby Adirondack Mountains, along the boundary waters of the northern Midwest, and out across the spectacularly carved canyon lands of the Southwest. Caro explained that Moses's leverage over Harriman was that he could manipulate media images of both of them at will. By controlling powerful images of public works around the state, Moses could either reward the governor for good behavior by including him in his P.R. efforts, or he could punish him for bad behavior by ignoring him or casting him as an opponent to the public good. In Moses's own book, he said that Averell Harriman "was a notably intelligent, hardworking governor, but

somehow he could not, to use an overworked cliché, project
his image. He was inept in his relations with press, air [radio
and television], politicians, and the general public. He was
handicapped by aloofness and modesty."[21]

In a battle of media images, the little people along the river
stood in the way of progress. One may not build with metaphors, as Moses declared to the Canadian Club of Ottawa, but
it was clear that one used metaphors to grasp and maintain
the authority to build—in this instance, to grasp and maintain the authority to fire up the bulldozers along the pristine
shores of the St. Lawrence.

july 1, 1958

The polar opposite of Massena's 1952 sesquicentennial movie
is an amateur production made by a man who worked on the
river during the 1950s. Dan Henry was a watchman for the old
Alcoa power plant who apparently carried a color movie camera with him to work for several years. He thought it might be
nice for his family and friends to have a glimpse of the river as
it was before the Seaway, during its construction, and on the
days when the water rose as the Seaway was opened. The latter
started with what the papers called Inundation Day, the mo-
mentous celebration of flooding that began on Canada's Do-
minion Day, July 1, 1958, and lasted three days until America's
Independence Day on the fourth.

For several years before that moment when the coffer
dams were blown up enabling the vast new lakes to begin filling, Dan Henry documented the river in the same pastel col-
ors we see in the 1952 anniversary film. But while the latter
was intended to be congratulatory, optimistic, and ambitious,
the Henry home movie provides a wistful, at times resigned
glimpse of what was and what had to be. Some years after he

shot the footage, Henry realized that many people had forgotten what the river had been like and might want to see how it had changed. So he recorded a commentary to accompany his silent images and his home movies were turned into a film about the river during the great project.[22]

After he showed scenes of local men working on the river in the final months before the Seaway construction began, it all began to change as other men with heavy equipment took the land. It started with the chain saws. Down came the trees: the big ones that somehow survived the early settlers and then all of the rest that had grown up in the intervening years to provide shade for those who lived and worked along the shore. His camera came up close to a tree limb lying across the ground still holding an intact nest of young birds. The mother was gone. "Somebody said, 'They'd better learn to fly quick,'" Dan remembered. By then the river people must have been gone too from their homes, farms, and cottages for miles up and down the river, because once the trees were cut, the bulldozers began their work, pushing the timber and the brush into giant piles to be torched. Dan's camera panned vast stretches of rolling pale-green grasses dotted with fires flaring across the horizon, a gray haze of smoke hanging over it all.

Then the buildings started to go. One day at work Dan noticed a huge conflagration on the horizon, so he headed out toward it with his camera. When he got closer he discovered buildings burning out of control, flames higher than the roof peaks whipping in the wind. No fear of spreading wildfires here; it all needed to burn. "It started looking different pret' near every day," said Dan. "The trees were going and buildings being burnt and . . . my God."

His camera revealed how in the winter the bulldozers approached the fine old farmhouses and barns with long steel cables to systematically destroy the buildings. First they ran the cables through the windows and attached them to a bulldozer so it could rip the cables through all of the vertical posts holding up the first floor of the house. The dozers would then turn around and knock out two of the building's adjacent corners and slowly the structure would start to go, shifting, shifting, then quickly falling off to one side, cracking under its own weight, slumped down and broken.

The film shows barns emitting thick white smoke, a blaze having been started inside. Suddenly the heat reached the critical point and the inferno broke through every window, every crack, transforming the structure from dull gray into a bright orange funeral pyre. Then the crushed farmhouse was lit. It went up quickly and violently. I thought as I watched this scene how close my house had come to that flash point forty years later; how my neighbor Lynn had carried his video camera so my wife and I could remember too. A little while later Dan Henry's camera returned to the farmhouse when all that was left was a fireplace and chimney amid a few smoking, blackened sticks. Recalling the scene, he told us how much he had hated to see those old farmhouses go. They were made of such beautiful timber, he said, a hundred years old. Just up the river from that farmhouse, Louisville Landing existed no more.

But the cutting and burning was not all. The entire landscape was denuded. Tom Vallance's once fertile Croil's Island sat low and brown in the background while the mainland shore was a rutted, muddy expanse. As Dan watched one panoramic shot that revealed the utter barrenness of the landscape, he talked as if in the intervening years he'd forgotten what had been done to the land. "Boy, that looks different right there, from the way I remember things." Fortunately for him, his memories of the river remained from before the destruction. Then, as he watched them take down buildings where he had worked for years, he said, "If the Seaway hadn't come along I'd a probably stayed there until I retired. But," he paused, "you can't stop progress." And at the very end, he repeated the mantra. "You can't stop progress," he concluded, "but we loved the old river out there."

While stripping the land of all life was a large project, stopping the flow of the river, in particular the raging current of the Long Sault Rapids, the heart of the river's impediment to commercial exploitation, was among the most difficult tasks. Dan showed us how it happened, as giant shovels and dump trucks on both sides of the river dropped load after load of stone across the head of the rapids until only a narrow but ferocious gap remained. Finally, after repeated efforts to plug the gap by a variety of methods, the two sides were connected and the coffer dam held. The legendary rapids were silent. Later we saw Dan and his family hopping about excitedly among the boulders and across the large slabs of stone that had made the river there so dangerous. Hundreds of others, according to Carleton Mabee, went down to see the rapids laid bare: "The more adventurous walked over the two-mile-long rapids bed, and decided the rocks were not so big as the size of the waves had led them to expect. . . . Zoologists poked about the potholes to pick up rare specimens of minute creatures that had lived under deep, swift water. Scavengers found wooden beams and iron ship plates wedged under rocks, and wondered what tragedy might lie behind them. A Sheek Island farm boy hauled out eleven cannon balls, perhaps from the War of 1812, and nearly fought another war with the Ontario government over his right to keep them."[23] The heads of both the Canadian and New York power agencies visited the site too, and after seeing the result, announced that any doubts about their ability to build the giant power plant had been eliminated.[24]

The once wild river would now be controlled, its dangers and uncertainties managed.

Yet the process of gaining this advantage over the river was costly. The monetary price tag was highly publicized because it reached an unprecedented level, one billion dollars. A popular commemorative booklet didn't even need to include the names St. Lawrence or Seaway in its title. It was simply *The Billion Dollar Story*. Anyone who was interested in the Seaway in 1959 would know what story that was. But less trumpeted was the human cost. While the number of deaths incurred during the construction was made public, it was accompanied by explanations of how comparatively safe the project had been. For example, a Toronto paper noted that while a total of forty-two workers on both sides of the border lost their lives during the construction, this number compared favorably with the average of sixty construction deaths each in the building of the Panama Canal, Golden Gate Bridge, Hoover Dam, and Empire State Building.[25] The number of injuries, however, was difficult to determine. Mabee illustrated the dangers of the undertaking when he described the struggle to close off the Long Sault Rapids. After a cable slipped and whipsawed one man's leg off and severely injured another's, the workers, according to Mabee, began calling the rapids "Cripple Creek."[26]

Other workers told tales far more graphic than any recorded at the time. Stories persist that at least one man fell into one of the great concrete pours and became entombed in the structure. But such stories have more the ring of myth than truth. Undoubtedly, though, there were some grisly scenes. For example, as work to build the huge monolithic structures that would serve as the walls of the locks and dams proceeded twenty-four hours a day, dangers increased. One man working a late shift reached out to turn on a large electric light. He was wearing leather boots that had gotten wet. Somehow he grasped an uninsulated wire and was electrocuted. When the doctor arrived, the foreman had been administering artificial respiration for about thirty minutes. About forty men stood around them as the doctor asked the foreman to roll the man over. Not realizing what would happen next, the foreman held the man's head in his hands between his knees as the doctor pulled out a scalpel and proceeded to slice the man open so that he could manually massage his heart. Workers all around started backing away. Some became sick. By the time the doctor pronounced him dead, only the foreman remained.[27]

But neither the loss of life nor the losses of the dispossessed nor the lost wild rapids nor the lost villages intruded on the excitement of Inundation Day. This would be the first day of a new era not only for the Great Lakes and Canadian shipping, not only for power consumers across the northeast, but also for the north country. Hailed by local papers as one of the most historic and dramatic occasions in the history of the St. Lawrence Valley, it was actually a slow event. Dan Henry's film shows his family walking down old roads to meet the water as it crept toward them, his kids standing on the edge and jumping back laughing against the inexorable rise. By then the landscape of the river needed something to return it to beauty. Only when the water rose to its new levels would the scars of destruction be covered; only then would the shore be lined with trees and green fields. Only then would they have a river again.

But, of course, it was a very different river. Fluctuating water levels played havoc with the ecology of the new shoreline. And while the impediment of the great rapids was overcome for shipping, the fish faced new impediments in the giant dams. Over time locals would discover that the bountiful fishing was gone forever. Over time they would discover that while there were some benefits for the north country—two new industrial plants brought jobs (as well as damage to the ecosystem through the introduction of new pollutants); some Seaway jobs were created; some tourism dollars were generated (which eventually withered as the novelty of the Seaway faded); some new commerce developed at the Port of Ogdensburg; a massive amount of electric power was generated (though most of it was sold to the aluminum producers or private power companies, leaving very little for cheap, local municipal power)—given these developments, the promise of the Seaway for those who lived near its final bottleneck had been largely oversold.

Even so, the power was needed—and today that need is growing steadily. Currently, as the northeastern states are supporting federal government efforts to curb emissions on coalburning midwestern power plants which generate acid rain that falls across the forests and lakes of New York and New England, hydropower is often touted as a less destructive way to meet growing power needs.[28] That northeasterners are stretching the limits of power generation capacity across the region is clear. "Power demand is rising faster than the systems' ability to generate and deliver it," read a front-page story in the New York Times after a heat wave in the summer of 1999 resulted in the greatest demands ever on power systems across the northeast. This increased consumption, "driven by a booming economy and the proliferation of computers, fax machines, air-conditioners and the other amenities of an affluent, wired society," is driving the construction of the first new power-generating facilities in New York in decades. Similar developments are happening across the nation.[29] Within two weeks of that record demand, U.S. Energy Secretary Bill Richardson announced a six-point plan designed to reduce the threat of weather-generated power outages. That plan included efforts to study the nation's present and future ability to meet electric power demands and to spur the development of new power generation and transmission technologies. In a speech on the issue Richardson said that power outages are a matter of life and death and people should not have to worry about the stability of the power grid every time demand goes up.[30] A year later, however, the same threat of power outages loomed over the nation's large urban centers as the summer began to heat up. By the end of 2000 the power grid in California was on the verge of collapse, with no easy solution in sight.[31]

In contrast, at the same time there were national news reports on a growing movement to take down power dams across the United States.[32] In response to environmental concerns, federal agencies were promoting the dismantling of power dams in which the environmental remediation costs outweighed the revenue generated by the hydropower. In describing a variety of dams in jeopardy across the nation, these reports were consistent with the conclusion published three years earlier in Patrick McCully's *Silenced Rivers,* which argued that an international antidam movement had effectively turned the tide against the construction and maintenance of big dams. Speaking of dams that have displaced or could displace hundreds of thousands of people, McCully showed that with the global rise of democracy, concerns for self-determination of indigenous people, more effective communications technologies, and international environmental movements, what was once inevitable is now in decline. "Activists working at the local, national, and international levels have together managed to tarnish seriously the lure of large dams as icons of progress and plenty," he wrote. "To many people, big dams have instead become symbols of the destruction of the natural world and the corruption and arrogance of over-powerful and secretive corporations, bureaucracies, and governments. . . . The international dam industry appears to be entering a recession from which it may never escape."[33] When the Moses-Saunders Power Dam was agreed to in 1953, it was granted a license to operate for fifty years. As I write this, negotiations on its relicensing for 2003 are ongoing. While a variety of local interests are negotiating with the Power Authority for changes in the way the project operates or the benefits from the sale of power are distributed, eliminating the power dam or reducing the amount of power it generates are most definitely not among the options. There's no going back. The giant dam and the obliterated, drowned old villages are a permanent part of the landscape.

Like Franklin Hough's tale of "unavailing regret" at the loss of four members of the frontier community of Louisville, an account written a hundred years later by fellow historian Carleton Mabee recounted another story of a man in danger on the river: "Seeing all the past he knew being shaved off the landscape, a retired farmer of Aultsville, Ontario, in his eighties, grew lonely. One day, taking a last chance to recover his past, he took a boat to row over to one of the islands where he had lived on a farm as a child, an island that would soon be largely submerged. A few days later his body was recovered from the river. He was disturbed by the destruction around him, explained a daughter."[34] On Inundation Day the waters began to rise over the land inhabited for millennia by its first peoples, over Louisville Landing and the farms of those early settlers who dispossessed the first peoples while carving out a life in the wilderness for their own families and fighting to defend their nation's new borders, over places that were once important but were quickly forgotten, over a quiet way of life. This was just part of the price some have paid for an addiction to all that power.

five the grid rebuilt

friday, january 9, through the end of january 1998

Al Bradley drove out across the frozen Seaway valley to see for himself. When he got to the transmission lines coming from the big hydropower systems, he knew the region was in trouble. He saw three of the big towers that carried power into the Niagara Mohawk system snapped in half. They were well off the road, and it would take a tracked vehicle to get in there to begin working on them. And this was just one little problem, he thought; the transmission grids were in trouble, and the substations were dark everywhere.

The complex system that feeds the power addiction had broken down. Of course to call the need for power an addiction is like calling the need for oxygen an addiction. Very few of us live and work outside the realm of electrified technology. Even for those who go off the grid or consciously try to simplify and detechnologize their lives, living without any electric power is nearly impossible. Large-scale food production and distribution, shelter production and distribution, many forms of play, and almost all forms of work require power that finds its source either directly or indirectly in the electric grid. Like it or not, it is the foundation for modern life. And that foundation was undermined in a profound way across vast stretches of

Ontario, New York, Quebec, Vermont, New Hampshire, Maine, New Brunswick, and Nova Scotia in the second week of January 1998. Unlike the focused, piercing devastation of a tornado, hurricane, flood, or earthquake, this event took a week to evolve as it slowly, incrementally compressed the power grid past the breaking point. The heaviest accumulations covered the Seaway valley from its source at the eastern edge of Lake Ontario across a wide path north and south of the river all the way past Montreal. When the rain finally stopped falling, those lands were under more than four inches of ice.

Although all disasters have their unique dangers, in many ways the impact of the ice storm was less a sudden catastrophe than an unforeseen change in the way we had to live. Many other types of disasters leave relatively clear boundaries between destruction and normality. For those who are fortunate enough to emerge safely from the mayhem of, say, an earthquake or tornado, escape is possible. The path of destruction is narrow and capricious. One person's world may be destroyed while a neighbor's goes untouched. Or in the case of all but the largest of hurricanes, a section of a town may be obliterated while other parts survive largely intact. There is some level of destruction and some level of normal living, and the distinction is clear. In contrast, the ice storm was far less violent, far less lethal, but far more democratic; it afflicted everyone within its vast boundaries. And for most of those five million people, there was no escape. The only option was to adapt and endure.

But endurance left many of us in an odd state, not wanting, of course, to live under disaster conditions but strangely at a loss when power was finally restored. Why was the experience at once traumatic and enlightening, untenable yet rejuvenating? What did we see when we saw ourselves in the media mirror and how did our unique experiences compare to the image we became? Why were we left so strangely unsettled when the grid to which we are inextricably bound was finally restored?

In the darkness of the broken grid, Marge Howe needed help. Her friend Hubie was still gasping for oxygen in the wee hours of the morning of Friday the ninth, while the full tank that could not operate without electricity sat untapped in the next room. Hubie's portable, nonelectric tank was nearly empty. At 2:30 A.M. the phone finally rang. The woman from the hospice had located a new tank and the sheriff's patrol would be bringing it out. When Marge told Hubie, he began to calm down. She turned on a battery-powered lamp and they waited. The key was keeping Hubie as relaxed as possible; lying awake in the dark could provoke the kind of night terrors that strike even the healthy.

Nearly an hour later a car pulled up outside. A man from the sheriff's patrol carried in a small tank of oxygen. "Great," said Marge, "can you hook it up for us?" He didn't know how and neither did Marge. "They just told me to bring the oxygen," he said, "I have no idea how it works." Marge told him leave it; she'd figure something out.

She called the Hannawa Falls Fire Department and asked for Janet Brown, but she wasn't there so Marge explained the problem. She said that Hubie's tank had maybe enough oxygen to last until six A.M.—if he stayed calm. Shortly after five Janet called to say that she would be over as soon as possible. She arrived by six and changed the depleted tank. Shortly thereafter the hospice called to tell Marge that they could not get anyone over there to stay with Hubie. Marge said she'd stay on, knowing full well that the new tank would last only so long. Somehow she needed to get to all that oxygen in the big tank.

She thought she had the answer when Hubie's son Bob called from Syracuse. As soon as the stores opened, he told her, he'd buy a generator and drive it to Potsdam. Marge told him that he'd have to talk his way through the roadblocks. A neighbor had told her that the day before a woman down the road who also helped out with Hubie had been trying to return to the north country from her vacation but had been turned back at the county line. Nonetheless, Bob made it through. What was supposed to be a three-hour drive wound up taking seven, but he arrived with a brand-new generator. Except that it wouldn't work.

By now Marge had had about twenty minutes' sleep in two days. Bob figured he had nothing to lose so he dialed the number of the Wal-Mart in Massena, not knowing whether it had power, was open, or had generators. Someone answered, and Bob explained their situation. No problem, he was told. If he could get there, they'd have one for him. A couple of hours later, Bob returned with another generator, and this one worked. Hubie was all set for oxygen. At 6 P.M. the fire department came, and Marge finally got a break. They drove her to her freezing-cold home, where she huddled under blankets trying to stay warm.

Patients on oxygen were only one of the problems facing Martha Hartle early Friday morning when she returned to the shelter at Potsdam State. Having been thrust in charge of the medical wing—a fieldhouse full of the sick and elderly, with more arriving continually—Martha needed to organize the few volunteers present to begin administering to the residents' considerable needs. With the indispensable help of Holly, a registered nurse who had arrived to volunteer her services, Martha and the other workers began to move about the floor. They soon discovered the complexity of the situation. They had epileptics. They had people on chemotherapy. They had a number of diabetics getting insulin but they had no way to check their blood sugar levels. They had a woman who needed to get to and from a dialysis facility thirty miles away in Ogdensburg. There were alcoholics who were beginning to exhibit withdrawal problems and psychotic patients whose behavior was causing concern. They had two pregnant women who were due to deliver. They had a number of people with respiratory problems, such as emphysema and asthma. They had a child with cerebral palsy. Some patients had to have dressings changed. They needed diapers, baby formula, baby food, adult Depends, and tampons. They had elderly who didn't understand what was happening. Many seniors couldn't get up off of the floor or walk to the restrooms without assistance. And no one, of course, wanted to be there. They were all worried about their homes and their fates. But they all seemed grateful for the help.

Martha needed more helpers, but until more volunteers arrived those who were there had to try to reach each patient. "I'd say, 'Okay, you take this part of the gym, and you take that part of the gym and try to find out what people need,'" Martha recalled later, "but people [residents] would leave. They'd be out wandering around. So you never really had a good idea of everyone and what their needs were. We didn't have a P.A. system. And trying to yell at the top of your lungs wasn't always effective." So the volunteers were constantly going from one patient to another to help with each person's needs. At some point there was ominous news about the storm from outside and it was spread across the floor by the volunteers in the form of a particularly unsettling question: "Do you have enough medication for ten days?" Not three days, but ten. This left people in shock. "What has happened to us?" The volunteers learned that they needed to do a lot of hugging and comforting, trying to keep people on an even keel.

They also had to keep people safely medicated, and Holly organized that operation. She communicated via cell phone with the hospital and then the local drugstores when they finally opened a couple of days into the storm. But Martha and the other volunteers could not legally administer medications, so they had to remind the residents to take their medications and then try to verify that they had. The volunteers soon discovered that some people had no idea what they were taking. " 'I take a blood pressure pill.' Well, do you know what it is? 'Well, it's a white pill about this big. I take it twice a day.' That was scary," recalled Martha, "it really was. We had a couple of instances. One woman got really confused. She had her medication with her in her purse and she lost track of time and had taken more of it than she should have." For a number of the elderly, the more time passed, the more confused they appeared. They didn't know if it was night or day or if they had taken their medication or not.

Over the course of the week many others had problems as well. At one point an alcoholic in withdrawal went into seizures. Others had sudden chest pains and had to be sent to the hospital. As soon as they were stabilized there, though, they were sent back to the shelter. The hospital was too crowded. But that didn't stop Martha from using the hospital as a last resort. One night, for example, a young woman who was anorexic and bulimic seemed to be very sick and one of the other residents alerted Martha, urging her to do something to help the woman. "I sat there and spoon-fed her," said Martha. "I said, 'Look, I don't have the time or energy for this so you can either eat or I'll call the ambulance and you can go to the hospital. And if you don't want to go in the ambulance, then the police will take you.' And I said, 'If I see you put your finger in your mouth, you're in trouble.' She didn't." One day the shelter ran out of food except for white rice, and that's all some people were served.

Another night a man who was diabetic decided he couldn't stand the shelter any longer. He had had enough of all the people and all the difficulties and he just left. He had no medication and no jacket. The police spent three hours looking for him and found him all the way across town at his own freezing home covered up in bed. His temperature had dropped and the police took him to the hospital. "But he was okay the next day," said Martha. "I could understand it. That's why I went home at night. He apologized. I said, 'Hey, you're not alone.' " Eventually some of the residents decided that there was a need for some quiet; people couldn't handle the constant noise. So Martha got on the bullhorn and announced that there would be quiet time twice a day. Everyone cooperated.

While life in the shelter afforded almost no privacy—health care, meals, and restrooms were all public—semiprivate enclaves evolved across the floor. For example, the seniors from one senior center congregated in one area while those from another had their own space as well. Those who came from private homes gathered around others whom they knew. While the overwhelming feeling was one of concern, Martha began to notice that many of the elderly, especially those who lived alone, seemed to be enjoying themselves in the open public square of their temporary home. And clearly many of the seniors wanted to help others; they kept an eye out for their neighbors, reminding them and the volunteers that their friend needed medication or help of some kind.

On Friday the ninth a local drugstore, Kinney's, delivered

a glucometer for the diabetics. On Saturday local physicians visited and the next day a variety of other support arrived: the National Guard, a medical unit from Fort Drum, the huge army base in northern New York, and representatives from the state health department. On Sunday church services were held. A Catholic priest and a Protestant minister led services and an African American gospel group sang spirituals. A piano was brought in to the seniors area and played by a local lawyer. By then Martha felt that the ad hoc system of caring for the residents seemed to be working. There was a regularity developing in the facility that seemed reassuring to all, residents and volunteers, even though the crisis on the outside was still quite intense.

A need for routine was what brought Judy Funston to the shelter. Waking up at her neighbor's home on Friday morning, Judy was restless. Her neighbor had mentioned to her that he might volunteer to work at the emergency shelter. The need for volunteers there had been one of the first messages broadcast when the local radio stations had come sputtering back to air; that and the ban on all nonemergency travel throughout the county. This was the first she'd heard about the shelter. All she knew was what she could see. No light, heat, or water at home; the welfare of her animals and plants threatened, with little she could do about it. But maybe the shelter was a way for her to get out. Maybe she could pack up her animals and plants and take them to her office across campus from the shelter. Her motivation was a bit selfish, she thought. "I was volunteering for the shelter because I just couldn't stay put. I had to be out. It gave me a reason to be on the road. I could drive into Potsdam."

Eventually Judy made it to campus and set up living facilities for her rabbit, cats, and plants in her office. The building was empty and without power but the temperature was holding at a livable fifty-five degrees. I shouldn't be here, she thought, but it seemed to work. That's when Judy began hearing announcements broadcast from a loudspeaker atop the Potsdam fire station: "Kerosene for sale at the fire station for one dollar a gallon, bring your containers; room at the shelter, bring your pillows and bedding, call this number for a ride." It all seemed so surreal: a voice echoing across this silent ghost village, most of its streets impassable, most of its residents shut up inside their homes trying to stay warm while she was hidden in her dark and deserted office building.

She walked to the campus public safety office and one of the officers drove her to the shelter, where she was directed to go upstairs to the seniors' area. That's where they really needed the most help, she was told. When she entered the large room and saw all the mattresses and cots, she was stunned. "People seemed very upset. There was a man in a wheelchair with his head in his hands sobbing. It didn't smell good. And I thought, What have I gotten into?" Her first job was to accompany a woman named Martha as she talked to people with medical problems. Judy recorded each interaction and listed each person's medical plan. Then she was told that the disabled women needed baths. "This was in a small, regular women's restroom, no windows, no lights. They gave me a towel for each woman and it was wet on one end. I was supposed to keep the other end dry. I had never worked with or been in close contact with elderly people, much less those with medical problems. The first woman I washed was an Alzheimer's patient. She kept pointing to the drain and asking if that was hers. I was just totally freaked out."

But she kept doing whatever she was asked. She helped people go to the bathroom. She got food for those who couldn't walk. She helped people shake out their bedding and tidy up their areas. "I felt that would probably make them feel more together if their little space was nice. And they really appreciated it." Eventually she was told that they needed her mornings at six to help everyone wake up and go to the bathroom and such, and then later each evening, when they put people to bed.

For the first few nights she slept in her office. But it started to bother her "to be in this cold, huge building in total blackness," so she ended up sleeping at a friend's house some miles away. Her life developed a much-needed routine. She worked mornings and evenings at the shelter. She spent the afternoons trying to keep her life together: checking in on her fish, taking care of the animals, getting more clothes from home. And every morning she automatically went upstairs and worked with the same people. "I know in my life it is important to have routine and continuity, and I thought that a familiar face would be important to them," she said. Yet despite the growing regularity of her days, she still felt disoriented.

The strange thing about this whole experience was that I felt divided in several ways. On one end of the spectrum I was heartbroken to see the destruction, to see my trees destroyed, to see my plants die, my house becoming increasingly colder, now a shell with everything basically taken out. I was sleeping in Norwood, my fish were down the road. My animals and plants were in my office. And I'm very much a home territory sort of person. I love being by myself in my house. I felt very dislocated.

But the other end of the spectrum was being so totally blown away by how people pitched in and were so incredibly kind and caring, how the community pulled together. People from Massena sent home-made cookies one night. People who could play musical instruments would come in and give little concerts. Clowns would come in for the kids and juggle. I wanted to cry because of all of the destruction and terrible dislocation, and I wanted to cry by being so moved by what people were capable of.

And in the middle of all that, I watched this whole organism in the gym become transformed, how it changed over the days. At first when I was sort of plopped in there, it was very chaotic. People had just arrived. They were needing medication. They didn't know what pills they had, and so we had to get doctors. It was all very disorganized. Several days later the gym had been arranged into sectors. There was a med chart for each person in the sector, and it was alphabetized within each sector, and there was a table for medications and a table for food. It was very organized. I also noticed that there were little neighborhoods, and people would go visiting from table to table. There were little communities within the larger community.

Judy became particularly attached to one elderly couple. The wife suffered from Alzheimer's and the husband took care of her. "During the days the wife would want to walk, so I would take her around and around. And she would tell me all these stories. The first story she told me, she said, 'I went out to the garage last night and I was laying things out, and I saw a man over there and he was just smiling at me. I didn't mind. I wasn't scared. I just kept doing what I had to do.' " As Judy listened carefully, the images seemed to her like a description of a painting by Magritte. "She thought I was the little girl who grew up across the street from her. She kept telling me how much she loved me and my sister. One of these summers she was going to teach me how to dance." There was Judy, who valued order, routine, cleanliness, and solitude, thrust into a messy, crowded, chaotic, and surreal world. Over time, as one of the other volunteers said to her, it all became addictive.

After a few days the shelter was operating at near capacity and this left a very difficult decision for the town supervisors and police. To them, the scope of the disaster was becoming clearer. From Lake Ontario to the North Atlantic there were thousands of shelters and millions of people without power. National emergencies were declared on both sides of the border. Utility crews were driving from all across both countries to enter this vast zone of darkness. The interstates into the disaster were becoming a parade of utility trucks. The number of power poles needed would soon deplete national stockpiles. Decision makers at the power companies were beginning to predict that the crisis could last for weeks. And the weather was getting cold again, bitter cold. Significant snow was in the forecast. Town officials were trying to decide how they could operate under emergency conditions, maintain a travel ban, seize and reserve supplies of gasoline for emergency needs, and still keep the bulk of the population safe *in their own homes*. That was the key. People had to be able to fend for themselves without normal services and without intruding on emergency services. With no working traffic lights, for example, local officials didn't want lots of nonessential traffic darting about on unsafe roads. Small catastrophes could start to proliferate. At the same time they wanted to let people get out to do whatever was necessary to survive. So they opted to finesse the travel ban. Yes, nonessential travel was forbidden and yes, citations would be given to those who flouted this directive, but officials would also be sensitive to people's needs. While there was no official announcement, word started to spread that local travel was possible. And three things would soon be sought after by almost everybody: food, water, and fuel. Of the three, fuel was the most coveted item.

A plan to get some gasoline into the north country was on the mind of my brother-in-law, Steve, on that first Friday of the storm. Calling from one of the service stations he owns downstate, he seemed to know more about what was happening than we did. "What have you heard?" Kath asked. According to news reports, he told her, the storm was huge and power might not be restored for quite a while. He said that they were having problems in Maine. Kath was surprised. "Maine?" I heard her say. We weren't sure if the power was out beyond the next town, much less all the way to Maine. He knew we didn't have a generator but he had an idea. He said that he'd be willing to fill a fifty-five-gallon drum with gasoline and drive up with that and his generator.

We were somewhat taken aback by this proposal. Steve isn't one to exaggerate, but it couldn't be that bad. The power would be back anytime now, I thought. It always is. I mean, you can't just wake up one morning and have to live off of a generator for the foreseeable future. That doesn't happen. Kath thanked him for the offer but said she didn't think we'd need it. We'd get back to him, though, if things started looking bad.

Although we didn't realize it just then, our neighbors had already begun searching for fuel. Lynn and Shirley Warden's generator needed to be fed. Their son Mike and Dave Centofanti from across the road were going to defy the travel ban and look for gas. If they got stopped, they'd just say that they were trying to find fuel for a generator that was keeping several families warm. Certainly the police would see that as essential emergency travel, they figured. By then both Mike's and Dave's families had decided to abandon their increasingly cold homes for Lynn and Shirley's. Other neighbors had stopped by too. One was looking for wood to burn in his fireplace. But none of us had firewood anymore.

Mike and Dave found some gas at one station in Potsdam that was running its pumps by generator. They filled a few small gas cans but then spilled some of it in Mike's van on the way home. They went back later with more cans but someone at the station said they had run out of gas. The next day that same station was selling again but limiting purchases to five dollars per person. The owner said he had to save most of his supply for official emergency vehicles. By then they had found a few larger gas cans—I had added mine to the pile—and Dave knew of a little station out in the country that just might be selling gas to anyone. So the two of them headed out of town in Dave's truck. But the main road was blocked by dozens of utility trucks surrounding a large substation. Not knowing how long they would be held up, Dave said he knew another way to the station but they'd have to take a back road, which, after some maneuvering, they were able to reach. Once they started down that road, Dave didn't want to stop or slow down. It was in very bad shape. Even though there was evidence that others had gone through, they still had to dodge downed and falling trees; it was icy and slippery and covered with big pot-holes, some of which were full of water. Dave was afraid he'd get into one of those holes and not make it back out. So he didn't slow down. "It was like WADOOM! and you'd come out of it. Pretty hard on the truck." At one point when they were snaking through a tunnel of large fallen trees, he hit a branch and cracked the windshield. He was worried that they'd get stuck out there and it would be hours before someone else came down that road. That would make for a long, long walk home. "And we weren't supposed to be out on the road anyway. It felt like we were moonshiners." Finally they made it to the station only to find that the word about it had gotten out. They waited in line for twenty minutes but were able to fill the rest of the cans.

By this time Kath and I had decided to take Steve up on his offer. The only question was, Could he make it through roadblocks? We called the state police and all they would tell us was that nonofficial travel was forbidden. So Steve decided that with a generator and drum in the back of his pickup and the flashing yellow emergency light he had on the top, he'd be able to make it through. And at midday on Saturday he and Kath's father, Bob, drove north through the Adirondacks to Potsdam. When they arrived, we were curious to know what it was like "out there." Kath's father said there was a sharp line of destruction that they had passed into as they descended out of the mountains some miles south of town. After that point, he said, the utter destruction of the trees reminded him of photos of European forests in World War II that had been shelled—as far as he could see there were just tall sticks with craggy, broken branches drooping down. Kath and her old man wired the generator into our furnace and water pump, which together would pretty much max out its capacity. They set it up so that it could be disengaged and carried over to Dave's house intermittently to keep his pipes from freezing too.

With this, the experience began to change for me. It was becoming clear that the power wasn't just about to come back. We were all starting to realize that we were in the middle of a disaster and we'd better be prepared to take care of ourselves. After Steve and Bob left, Kath and I decided to empty the refrigerator and set up a makeshift one on our back deck, which had the effect of putting all our perishables in a freezer. We also decided to join the Wardens and the Centofantis in cooking supper at the Wardens' house. The four families would pool some key resources. I heard myself saying things like, "Let's see, with that fifty-five gallons of gas, the twenty-five you have in those cans, the other fifty or sixty gallons we have left in the tanks of all our vehicles, we'll be alright." Twenty-four hours earlier the storm was merely an annoyance that was keeping me from finishing my course syllabi for the coming semester. Suddenly I'm talking about siphoning off gas tanks so we don't freeze; suddenly I find that we're making decisions like having the kids stay in the Wardens' rec room because it was the warmest spot in all our houses.

For me this was an ironic and deserved fate. Here I was, a guy who a couple of years before had written a book that touted local life while warning people of the potential dangers of spending too much time connected to global networks— and all the while I was continually connected to such networks, all the while I was participating in global discussions about local living; that's the kind of thing academics typically get paid to do. Now my network extended across one yard to the Wardens' house and across one road to the Centofantis' house. No matter how often I had preached about the importance of geophysical place before, I had never in my adult life been so totally consumed for so long by such a limited here and now. It was a moment-by-moment existence devoted to the people and property around me, punctuated intermittently by a collective story being told by the local radio stations. And when I look back at all the stories that have been written locally about this experience—those, for example, presented in a variety of postdisaster, special edition newspapers or told on several collector's edition videos—I see a common message:

across the region a grid of social ties, formal and informal, organized and serendipitous, public and private, official and ad hoc, arose spontaneously in place of the lost power grid.

Lynn Warden's experience, for example, represents a kind of cross section of that amorphous social grid. As the head of security for the regional Kinney's drugstore chain, Lynn knows well all aspects of that business. He knows how stores operate, from the ways inventories are managed to the ways employees carry out each transaction. He also knows how closely community health is tied to the commerce of the local pharmacies. On Friday the ninth Lynn got a call from the manager of the Potsdam store, who said he had lined up a few people and they were going to try to open for business for a few hours. It would be announced on the radio. That's when we first started to wonder about the travel ban. If they're announcing that the drugstore is open for prescriptions, then we have to be able to travel, right? Lynn said he'd be over. All seemed okay at home. The generator was running. The basement was warm. Mike and Dave were starting to find gas. The kids were having fun in the rec room and Mike and Marge's new baby wasn't due for a week.

Because the shelter at the university was in dire need of pharmaceuticals, one of the local fire departments had dropped off a small generator at Kinney's that morning. With that they were able to run the pharmacy computer, which was crucial because it held the records of all their customers' prescriptions. So when, say, one of the elderly at the shelter couldn't name his or her medication, the store would be able to pinpoint it. There were no lights on in the store nor were the cash registers powered.

Even though the local radio stations were on air only intermittently, the word spread and by midday a line had formed outside the store. Each customer was escorted through the darkened building by an employee with a flashlight. In addition, calls were coming in from the shelter for prescriptions and the police and volunteer fire department people were serving as couriers. At the end of the day, Lynn also made a few deliveries to some local homes and to the shelter. But for the six hours it was open, the store sold far more than just prescriptions. It sold out of batteries and candles. Also popular were baby supplies, any kind of food, and a variety of over-the-counter medications. All transactions were tabulated on a hand-held calculator and written in a notebook. This is the way stores across the region operated every day until power was restored.

On Saturday one of the local supermarkets opened under the same conditions, and Dave and I drove over and got in line outside. It was my first trip out since before the storm and I was unnerved by the destruction to the trees and by the sight of people looking into the windows of closed gas stations trying to see if anyone was inside. It was also a bit unnerving to shop this way. By then the temperature had dropped into the teens and I was thinking I had seen this on T.V. before: Brezhnev-era Muscovites lined up in the freezing Russian winters to enter empty markets to buy a loaf of bread and piece of mutton. While this wasn't an empty supermarket, it was a rather spooky one. Dave and I went in together with our escort, grabbed two shopping carts and started perusing the aisles in the muffled darkness cut only by five or six flashlight beams bouncing about the cavernous room. Suddenly, several men in hardhats with clipboards came bursting through the line and, without explanation, began grabbing all the meat they saw in any customer's cart and tossing it into a big bin on wheels. I didn't know who they were but the message was clear. Don't touch the meat.

This kind of operation was good for the first day or so, but these stores would need to be resupplied, especially with the key items: medications, bottled water, baby formula, batteries, and candles. So while Dave and I were haunting the supermarket aisles, Lynn drove over to the local Kinney's to make a list of items they needed, stopped back home to pick up Shirley's cell phone so he'd have some line of communication, and then he and another corporate manager headed out of town to the corporate distribution center in the town of Gouverneur, thirty-five miles to the southwest. "That really opened my eyes," he said later. "That was the first time I had any opportunity to really see the magnitude of the destruction. I had never seen anything like it before. As soon as I headed out of Potsdam toward Canton, power pole after power pole after power pole was snapped off. One would have to see it to believe it. There were some places where I think in a three-mile stretch, two power poles were standing. I'd guess that maybe 70 percent of the power poles between Canton and Gouverneur were down."

The purpose of the trip was twofold. First, he and the other corporate managers had to try to put together some kind of game plan to get supplies out of the central warehouse to the stores across the region. Second, Lynn and his colleague planned to drive a truck back north full of supplies for as many stores as they could reach. On the way to the distribution center they saw roadblocks, but no one stopped them. Route 11, the main artery across the north country, was clear. The side roads, however, were still treacherous. After they arrived they held a brief meeting, then the two of them found a loaded truck waiting for them and they started making the rounds to each store between there and Potsdam, which was the last town in the line. "We couldn't give everybody everything they wanted," said Lynn. "It couldn't be done. We'd call and say,

'We're coming.' We'd back up to the store. There was no set thing. We'd just try to divvy it up. We didn't have enough stuff to replace everything but it helped."

When Lynn returned home that Saturday night, he was greeted by a kitchen full of people eating a hodgepodge of food. Earlier, we had all gone through our respective food supplies and picked out the items that would be soonest to spoil and then cooked them all up on a motley collection of burners and camp stoves at each of our houses. The night before, Dave had grilled the rest of the venison that remained from a deer he'd shot a couple months earlier. "Here we are," Dave had said, "sitting around the campfire eating today's kill."

The first thing Lynn told us about was the destruction he'd seen along Route 11. His words sounded ominous. "So power's not coming back tonight?" I said, knowing the answer. No one needed to respond. By then most of us were exhausted. Lynn had spent much of the day before on his feet in the store; probably the longest stretch he'd ever had on his prosthetic leg. "There just wasn't a chance to sit down," he recalled. "How could you sit down with people out there wanting to come in?" Then on Saturday near the end of the delivery run, he'd stepped out of the truck onto some black ice and fell so hard that he snapped the handle off of a plastic coffee cup he had in his hand and also damaged the prosthesis. He could still use it, though.

The rest of us at home all seemed to have a number of things to do just to maintain the status quo. Kath and Dave and another man spent several hours draining the water from another neighbor's house that was uninhabited at the time. It had taken them the better part of an hour just to chip ice off the ground in front of the garage door so they could open it and get into the house. Later it took Dave and me that long to open our garage doors so we could get access to our cars. We also spent a lot of time either drawing water from our well or chipping ice to melt in buckets placed strategically around the Wardens' pellet stove. The ice melt was for flushing toilets. Our well water was for drinking.

In addition, we needed to move our generator around. It went back and forth between our house and the Centofantis', and one afternoon Dave, Lynn, and I drove it over to Mike and Marge's house in the village to pump out their basement, which had flooding problems and no operational sump pump. This was a common problem throughout the region. Just as we were carrying the generator back out to the truck, a woman who had appeared suddenly in the middle of the street looked at me and asked whether I knew of anyone who could spare a generator. She was nearly in tears. I hesitated. She said that there was a farm outside town where the cows were threatened because they couldn't be milked. I didn't know what to say. Our little generator certainly couldn't handle that job. Dave suggested she contact the police or fire department. Good Lord, I thought, are we going to find ourselves choosing between keeping our kids warm and fed or helping our neighbors save their livelihoods?

Back at the Wardens' house, the kids were being taken care of primarily by Cindy, Shirley, and Marge. My son and Marge's son, both just two years old, got easily upset at the absence of their parents. One time Cindy, who had just calmed Buck down, saw my boots descending the stairs as I went to get Lynn's tools from the basement. She called out, "If you're not planning to stay, GET OUT!" I quietly backed up the stairs and got tools elsewhere. Throughout these days, we were moving freely in and out of one another's houses. No one needed to knock; the houses had all become public places for the four families.

Because we could keep our house at around fifty degrees

with intermittent use of the generator, Kath and Buck and I slept there. And from our bedroom at around 5 A.M. Sunday the eleventh, we heard a car engine start up at the Wardens'. Kath and I looked out and saw what looked like the lights from Mike and Marge's van as it backed out of the driveway. We turned to each other. It can't be, we thought. She can't be having the baby now! An hour or so later, it was confirmed when I went over. Marge's water had broken in the wee hours and her doctor had told her to go to the hospital as soon as she could.

The hospital was running under generator power and, as Mike recalled later, when they arrived, it was like entering another country: all the lights worked, the bathrooms worked, it was warm. It was also crowded. Although there was a good chance that the baby would have to be delivered via C-section—their first had been—Marge's doctor could not schedule one until they were sure there was no other alternative. The operating rooms were under an emergency-surgery-only order. Marge would need to go into labor.

While these were powerful moments for the Warden family, they marked the beginning of a real roller coaster of experience for me. Later that Sunday morning Mike called his parents and asked if they could bring over some items they had forgotten to take with them. Kath and I volunteered to do it just as an excuse to get out. While we were in the hospital lobby, luxuriating in heat and light, I saw one of the administrators from Clarkson University, my employer. He told me that the campus center building had been set up as an emergency shelter and that the campus food service was providing food around the clock for anyone in the community who wanted to eat there. Clarkson was also providing sleeping facilities, unheated and unlit, for the increasing number of visiting utility workers, many of whom were working on twenty-four-hour schedules. The campus center was under generator power and there was a limited amount of hot showering available in the locker rooms of the adjoining hockey arena. That caught our interest.

When we got there we saw people on cots and rugs and makeshift beds all over the building, in every corner and section. In the middle was the dining hall area, which had a long buffet heaped with food. Kath said, "Let's eat lunch here." I said I didn't think we should. "This is for people who really need it. This is for refugees," I said quietly. "I'm not a refugee." Kath said that just because we could stand outside shivering by a Coleman stove and heat up a can of beans didn't mean we didn't need help too. We made ourselves some sandwiches but I felt funny about it. Later Kath took a shower there. When we got back to the Wardens', we told everyone about it and discussed whether we might all want to go there to eat sometime. But until they heard from Mike and Marge, Shirley and Lynn wanted to stay home by the phone.

By that Sunday evening we had all been without power for four days, and we had not seen any utility trucks working on our road, which was discouraging. But as Dave, Lynn, and I were bundled up and cooking on the camp stoves on Lynn's back porch, we noticed powerful lights in the darkness moving slowly up the road. Then they stopped. Dave and I decided to find out what was going on. A quarter mile down the road, a stretch that's all woods on either side, we came upon a couple of utility trucks patrolling the lines. We asked the guys how it was going and joked with them a bit. Dave invited them in to have some food or drink but they declined. They had to complete a certain number of circuits before they quit that night. Trying to keep the conversation going, Dave asked them where they were from and it turned out that one of the guys had gone to the same grade school as Dave had in Syracuse. Then Dave asked them the key question: Would they go over to his house and put up the downed service drop that had been torn off by some falling tree limbs? The foreman hesitated a bit but told him that before he went out again in the morning, he'd come over and see what he could do. I asked them if they had any idea when we'd get power and the foreman told me that the problem wasn't the distribution system—the wires on our road, for example—it was the transmission system. The big towers. "There are guys climbing all over those things trying to get that system back," he said. Until they did, no one would get power.

Once again, the prognosis was not good. And now the temperature was really dropping. After supper, Dave and I took the generator from his house back over to ours. It was clumsy, difficult work in zero-degree temperatures. Just carrying the unit over the ice, checking its oil and gas, and cranking it up was tiring. And it was starting to run raggedly, as well. Although we didn't know it at the time, people from New York to the Maritimes were learning about the dangers and difficulties of generators. First of all, generator exhaust was killing people. I heard on the radio that some people in the north country had been killed in their sleep by toxic fumes from a generator in their basement. Second, many of us were beginning to learn that your standard handyman's generator is not designed for the kind of strain this event was putting on them.

For some reason we couldn't seem to get the thing running. Kath, the engineer, checked it out, but she wasn't sure what the problem was. "It seems to be starved for fuel," she said. I looked to Dave. "I know how to fix some things," he said, "but this I don't know much about." Neither did I. Kath suggested I call her brother. It was getting late, but in this cold

I decided it wasn't unreasonable to call. His wife answered and said he was in Vermont playing hockey but that I should try his pager number. Twenty minutes later Steve called back from his truck somewhere in Vermont. He talked me through a check-out and told me he'd call back in a half hour to see how it went. It didn't go very well. During his second call, he told me how we could start tearing down parts of the engine to get at the carburetor. I wrote it down and went back out with Kath and Dave. By now it was sometime after ten and the temperature was well below zero. It was decision time. Should we try to do work we really didn't know how to do in conditions like these? I brought out the tools but Kath finally said that the house could hold its heat for one night. We could tackle it in the morning. We all agreed.

On Monday at dawn the temperature in the house was holding in the mid-forties. No frozen pipes as far as we could tell. Kath called in to work and was told they needed all the people they could get, so she headed north to Massena. I was very concerned about our situation. Steve's generator had been keeping two houses from deteriorating but I was afraid it wouldn't even start this morning. I burned some bread over the open flame of our camp stove, scraped some jelly across it and served it as toast to my son. He seemed happy so I called Lynn. I told him our generator had quit on us and I was worried about how we were going to keep things together. Lynn stopped me. "Steve. My generator is sitting in a pool of oil. It's dead."

I was stunned. We talked about it. He said he had a plan to get another one if he couldn't fix this one. I didn't say it but I was thinking, We're all going to end up in the shelter. I told him I'd be over shortly.

When we got there my son went off to play downstairs and Shirley told me that they had a new baby boy. They had gotten the word the night before. All had gone well. It was wonderful news and a tremendous relief. I congratulated her as Lynn hung up the phone. A friend of his was coming over to see if he could fix the generator. "But I've got another plan too," he said. His brother, who lived about five hours down-state, was going to meet Lynn in Syracuse with his own gener-ator. "Plus, I'm going to take this one back where I bought it and demand that they replace it." I've never been very good at that kind of confrontation so I wondered if they'd go for it. "They damn well better. But if they don't, we should see if we can fix this one." If I were Mike and Marge, I thought, I'd do all I could to stay in that hospital.

For the next several hours, Lynn, Dave, and I pored over that generator engine as if we knew what we were doing. We didn't, but eventually Lynn's friend Leo Grant showed up. Within an hour Leo, a state policeman who had taken time out from his duties to help us, had the thing running with a tem-porary repair. Then he walked over to my house and started messing with the carburetor. Eventually he showed me how to adjust the fuel and air mixtures, something I had needed to do as the temperature dropped. By the time Leo left, my genera-tor was purring right along. Later, Lynn headed out on his mis-sion to Syracuse, after Dave and I spent the better part of an hour chipping his truck out of the ice. Early in the evening Shirley got a call from him saying he was on his way back north with two generators and a load of groceries.

After five days without power, with Mike, Marge, and baby safely ensconced in the hospital, with one working gen-erator and two on the way, we all decided that we should treat ourselves by going to the Clarkson shelter to eat supper. And that event for me was the defining moment of the entire expe-rience.

To me the building that night evolved into a kind of place that has largely disappeared, even in small towns and villages; it became a public commons, a place where people met by chance and talked about whatever was on their minds. On this night, of course, conversations were focused. As one pushed a tray along the buffet line, the common question was "How are you doing?"—not the polite and empty how-are-you-doing but one that meant, What kind of heat do you have? How are you holding up? Who are you with? What have you seen? What do you know? The stories spilled out. Some people had generators, some had fireplaces or woodstoves. Those who had were sharing with those who didn't. Multigenerational families flung far across the region were coalescing at one location. Others, like us, found themselves throwing in with small neighborhood groups. Whole households were living in one room, the rest of the house closed off and abandoned to the cold. Some were enjoying the company, others were suffocating. For young kids it was fun, while teenagers were getting bored and difficult. There were stories about unexpected predicaments and amazing sights. There was grapevine information about the state of the power grid and who was going to get power first. People stood between tables holding trays of hot food getting cold and just kept talking. Or they leaned back in their chairs and talked over their shoulders to someone behind them. Attitudes ranged from a resigned relaxation to a kind of subdued, exhausted agitation. All were shocked by the state of the trees. At one point I realized that every one of the adults around that table—Kath, Shirley, Dave, Cindy, and myself—was turned away talking to a different person whom we may or may not have known. Talk was easy when everyone was bound by the same necessities. For me it was a simple but powerful night. We were all beginning to shape our collective experiences. We were discovering what the disaster meant. And while everyone's experiences differed in the particulars, they were also connected and similar.

Later that night I stood alone in our driveway, flashlight in hand, checking the oil level in the generator and thinking about some of the stories I had heard. The night was extremely cold again and my exposed fingers were getting numb, but I felt strangely good about the trip to the shelter. After filling the gas tank, I cranked the engine over and stood there in its roaring din, waiting for a moment before pressing the button to send the power down the line and into the house. Suddenly, I noticed something in the air falling through my flashlight beam. It can't be raining again, can it? I looked around and felt something pelting my face. Omigod, it's the oil. In my blissed-out, we're-all-in-this-together state, I had forgotten to screw the oil cap back on the generator and oil was shooting out all over me, the house, the truck, the ice. I was able to kill the engine seconds before completely depleting it of oil and frying it beyond repair. How quickly my mood could change. "I am freaking sick of this whole goddamn thing," I told Kath a few minutes later, as I tried to wash oil off my face and glasses with ice-cold water in the dark. "Sick of it. Completely."

Stress reduction, stories, and moral support became some of the most significant facets of North Country Public Radio's fare during the crisis. In fact the radio station became a kind of on-air public commons as it evolved. Yes, the station put lots of effort into gathering and relating crisis information, but it was the support function that became its most compelling feature.

After the first day or two of chaos, the reporters eventually developed an organized way to collect and announce information as their generator power stabilized. Early on they had little to pass along, then it started to tumble in and tumble out as the region began to cope with the initial crisis, and after a few days the information dissemination became quite systematic and regulated. There were plenty of choices to make, of course. For example, even though they ran a noncommercial station, for the first ten days or so they put a lot of commercial information out: so-and-so store is open and has generators, or a new shipment of kerosene is arriving at X gas station. The reporters recognized that there was a fine line between getting useful information out and running commercials. There were plenty of news items to track down too. The question of whether or not the county had seized all gasoline and kerosene supplies and controlled their distribution was a big story for a while. They also found themselves involved with one of the key contradictions of the event: they were continually an-nouncing the travel ban while simultaneously telling people where to go to buy supplies. When there was no news to re-port, they would call local experts on, say, operating generators or chain saws and do live interviews.

One of the most popular items had to do not with disaster technology but with disaster health. A local cardiologist came on a couple of times and discussed how to handle the stresses of the time. His manner was calm and reassuring. Mitch Teich remembered it as a segment on "emotional safety" as opposed to "chain-saw safety." But perhaps the most therapeutic pro-gramming of all was when they encouraged listeners to call in. "We discovered," said Mitch, "that people just wanted to talk. And while many of us could call relatives outside the region, there was something special about all of us in this shared expe-rience interacting across the region via call-in radio."

One night early on they were looking for something to fill the void, so Mitch did a call-in jazz show. Someone called with a top-ten list of ways he was enjoying the ice storm. They got a call from a nine-year-old talking about skating in his yard. "I remember someone calling in and saying they were really entertained by watching their cat chase around a pencil. We sort of realized that people were looking to channel all this adrenaline and all of these thoughts that were going around in their mind, and we were just giving them a way to think about it and express themselves."

Sunday night, January 11, was the first night the station featured open phones. Mitch suggested that people call in with their ice storm poems, and much to his astonishment they did. Then it became haikus, then limericks. "You could tell people to do things," said Mitch, "and they'd do it!"

He posed a question:

I said, "If you were the editor of *Life* magazine and you wanted to design a cover a year from now for a retrospective article on the ice storm, what one image stands out that you would put there?" And I threw out my image: On Saturday I drove to Ogdensburg, ostensibly to fill somebody's car up with gas but really it was to get out of the station for a couple of hours. I stopped at Burger King, which was a surreal experience because there was power and everything was going on as if it was normal, but you knew that something was really, really, really wrong because you knew that [in] Canton, nothing was normal. And I remember sitting there and eating my food and seeing at one point a convoy of eight utility trucks followed by five tree-trimming trucks from Dayton, Ohio, followed by a Ben & Jerry's ice cream truck. You know, here are the necessities of life. So I threw that out and people started calling up.

(Listening to Mitch tell this story reminded me of that van Kath and I had seen the first day, with the side door open and guys with chain saws sitting on the floor and dangling their legs out of the van as it passed. Had I been listening that night, perhaps that would have been my image. Or maybe it would have been the evening meal we attended at the shelter.)

The radio reporters were concerned that they might get some angry calls from people who thought the reporters were making light of things, but that didn't happen. Over time they got all sorts of calls, from the lighthearted to the serious, and the reporters treated them all with respect. And in the end they never got any calls that they thought inappropriate for the air. They had expected that maybe there'd be a teenager who realized, " 'Hey, I can say anything I want to and get away with it,' " said Mitch. "In fact teenagers did call. They were reading haikus!

"We and they needed a sounding board to say, 'Hey, it's okay, this is what everybody's doing and isn't this remarkable, we're getting through it.' People would call us from emergency shelters. And people would call us and we'd recommend them to go to the shelter. It was a way for people to reach out to others who were also going through the same thing. It became a shared experience rather than what it could have been, which was an awful, solitary suffering. It was just good to know that life was continuing in this place or that."

But what happened when the lights came back on and that shared experience was over? What happened to those social bonds once the emergency began to wane? For many of us that cohesion that had felt so real seemed to fade as the grid began to be reenergized. On the eighth day of the outage, Niagara Mohawk installed a large generator at North Country Public Radio. "I remember, the second the fluorescent lights went on in here, instantly there was a letdown," said Mitch

Teich. "And it was a weird kind of letdown: it was great to have these things come on. I knew the building would start getting warm. But at the same time I knew that there were other places that would not be getting power for another week or so and I'd never be able to empathize with them the same way as I did when we didn't have power. It was a real remarkable period of time that was now over. And it was much more difficult to keep running the station in crisis mode. We kept doing our emergency information but it was not the same."

On the night of Tuesday the thirteenth, after six days without power, a light over the stove in our kitchen suddenly came on. It stayed on. Later I would learn that we were among the first 30 percent to get power back in St. Lawrence County. After that, every day brought more people back online. It would take two more weeks to restore power to everyone in New York. It took until February 8, nearly five weeks after the storm hit, for the complete restoration of power in Quebec's "triangle of darkness" south of Montreal.[1]

In those latter days of the outage in New York, Al Bradley finally got a task that for him was gratifying. He had the opportunity to install large generators into facilities that needed them to serve the public: shelters, drugstores, food stores, and large restaurants where the visiting utility crews would be eating. "Some of those generators were owned by Niagara Mohawk, others came from the state, from FEMA, the Red Cross. We would install them if asked to. In those places, nothing yet was being turned on without a generator, so at least I got to see some happy people. It gave me a good feeling."

Because Al worked with a number of the visiting utility crews, he got to see the events through their eyes. They told him repeatedly that they were impressed with how friendly and cooperative the storm victims were. "A family might have been out of power for a week or two, but they treated the lines crews great and the crews really were gratified by that." Al quoted one lineman from an out-of-state utility who said, "By now where we work if we didn't have power back, we'd have smashed windshields. The people would be so hostile. The people here, twelve, one o'clock in the morning, we'd have the yellow lights flashing in their windows and out of the darkness comes women and children carrying food, coffee. Ask us if we want to come in and get warm. Can't believe it."

Those lineman had also never experienced the kind of widespread destruction they saw across the region. "We had guys here from the Southeast who have worked hurricanes and they said they're bad but the damage is concentrated to a relatively small area. They hadn't seen anything [affecting] this vast an area." Just as those lineman were impressed by the locals, Al and his fellow north country workers were amazed at the visitors' work ethic. "Those linemen from away seemed to care. Their families were safe at home watching this on television but I'd see them in the morning at breakfast and they'd say how frustrated they'd be, working three or four days round the clock and 'Haven't put one damn customer on yet.' " A colleague of Al's, John Gamble, who also directed visiting crews, saw similar things:

> It was heartwarming to see guys work so hard who didn't have a stake in it. They weren't doing it for themselves. The guys I worked with just wanted more and more everyday. "Give me a real job. Just give me a line to build." It was pretty easy directing people who were motivated. They knew people were hurting this time of year. You know, you go by houses, maybe they have a kerosene heater going. You know they're cold and hungry. You see a kid standing inside looking out a window. I've never seen men be so emotional. I

guess it's because the responsibility falls on your shoulders and there was a huge weight to bear. I saw guys in tears here. It was such a huge task and there was a lot of pressure on people to perform. I've worked with guys twenty-five years who were just devastated. We had guys driving here for sixteen hours ready to work and we'd send them out. People don't know what it took to get it done. Rain, sleet, snow, cold, wind. My outside crews slept for a week in a cold, dark motel room, the first two days on couches in the lobby, and no one complained. Never.

Recalled Al: "There were frustrations and triumphs, peaks and valleys, setbacks. But just over and over in my mind was those poor people. Those poor people have been out of power for two weeks. Food's all spoiled. Taking baths out of a pan. Terrible."

Within a couple of weeks all of us who had lost power would be back at work and school, our houses would be operating as they did before the storm, with one major task ahead of us after the spring thaw: cleaning up all the trees. But what many people soon discovered was that the experience was not over when the power came back on. As segments of the grid became energized every day, more and more people faced another unexpected change that came upon them as suddenly as the original outage.

"At the shelter you wanted to send people home," recalled Martha, "but those who were left behind felt bad. And those who went home felt guilty because they no longer were victims while others still were." Unfortunately for Martha, she felt bad for them all, and ultimately she felt a tremendous loss when the shelter finally closed. "The last few days were much harder emotionally than the first, even though those first days were more physically and mentally challenging."

Before the end, a state mental health official expressed amazement at how well the shelter volunteers had done with so many residents and so little help. "That person said to me, 'I've been watching and everybody just seems really fine. What are you doing?' I said, 'We're just doing a lot of hugging and putting arms around people.' I really encouraged that kind of contact. And a lot of those seniors were getting more attention than they usually get. We were concerned that when we'd send these people home they'd be lonely. We had people who didn't want to leave the shelter."

One day near the end, her boss, Clarkson's president, asked her to come in for a meeting. When she arrived, she couldn't focus on her job. The president asked her what was wrong, and she said she felt as though she needed to be at the shelter. He told her to go back to it. The following week, when she finally returned to work full time, she was depressed. She couldn't concentrate. She wanted to be with people who had gone through the same thing. "Because I didn't think that anyone could understand," she said.

"I feel like I've experienced posttraumatic stress syndrome. The second night we had power my husband came home, and I had the lights off and the candles lit, and he said, 'What are you doing?' and I said, 'I kind of miss the candles.' " Some months later she was still thinking about it. "I walked down the street, and it was a beautiful evening, and I kept thinking back to what it was like after the storm with the trees down and everything. I almost feel like I don't want to let go of that kind of image. I don't want myself or my family or anyone else to forget how terrible it was. One of the things that bothers me is that people who weren't here and people who don't know the north country think that, 'Well, an ice storm, you're used to that. An ice storm is nothing to you.' Because I've had people say that to me. They don't understand."

She also realized that this profound experience might not have happened to her had someone else been called. "I think it was divine providence because it really meant a lot to me. I don't really mean this, and you'll know what I mean when I say this, but I wish I could do it again. I'd love to have the opportunity to do it again because now I've got a dress rehearsal and I could even do it better. As a [rescue] squad member I always said I wanted to go to some big national disaster. In the Oklahoma City bombing I really wanted to go, but you know it's just not practical."

And yet while she had a vague desire to reexperience the event, she was well aware of the toll it had taken on people, the elderly in particular.

We've lost a lot of older people since the ice storm. Some people think that the ice storm had such an impact on the older people that they couldn't really recover. I don't know that it has actually been documented, it's just a sense I have. Other people have mentioned it too. One of the ladies who was at the shelter who I really took a liking to and fussed with, and she was so sweet, she just died last week and I was very upset by it because I hadn't gotten over to see her, and I really wanted to.

I've been going to church a lot more. I've felt that need. I've felt a real need for closeness to people. I have a hard time keeping in touch with people because I'm so busy. But during the ice storm, because everything stopped, there was time for making a lot of connections again. Now I almost feel as if I'm severed again from being with the people I want to be with because I don't have the time. The storm pointed out to me that my time is pretty well controlled by my job, and it has made me rethink that a lot, and I have made some changes, and I am continuing to make changes.

The ice storm put us all on the same level. No one was any better or worse. I think when people started getting their power back it started undoing that. For me I don't want to let go. I can feel it slipping away, and I don't want it to. My life always used to be "before my divorce" and "after my divorce," and now a lot of it is going to be "before the ice storm" and "after the ice storm." For me it's kind of a milestone event.

For Judy Funston the final days of the experience were also difficult. Shortly before the shelter was closed, Judy came down with a flu virus that had spread through the facility. Her home was still without power, and she was needed less and less at the shelter. She was torn by a variety of emotions. "I was in tears the last few days I worked there. People were leaving and it was coming to an end and I wouldn't see these people again. I admired them all so much. But by then all of these medical teams arrived and there were plenty of workers and I was just sort of standing around." One of the things she did as the work wound down was to take people home, which quickly became difficult because she found herself feeling somewhat jealous that they had power and she did not. Her electricity wasn't restored until the eighteenth, eleven days after the blackout began. In the end the strain of maintaining her home without power, enduring her sickness, and coping with the crash of emotions after quitting the shelter was devastating.

But after a period of recovery, she, like everyone else, picked up and resumed her prestorm life. She knew, however, that she had experienced a profound shift of perspective. Before she had been wrapped up in her academic world and took little notice of the nonacademic community. Afterward she started to feel a part of a particular place with particular people that went beyond the boundaries of her job. She also recognized that ordinary people like herself can do extraordinary and difficult things in a crisis. "I feel a different person. It has changed my view of human nature. It has changed my view of this community and what it means to belong to a community. I'm single and I feel myself to be somewhat of a loner. That hasn't changed, but I feel now a part of this community in a way that I hadn't before. My only regret is that I couldn't have done this sooner.

"It has changed my view of myself. I'm proud of what I did even though it started with my selfish motive. But I surprised myself. You know, when the stomach flu was going around, people were having diarrhea and throwing up. But I kept thinking all the time, What if I were in this position? I would want to keep clean. I would want to have help. And my response surprised me."

Her experience also changed her view of the elderly. Before the storm she was mostly oblivious to the elderly in the community, maybe at times dismissive or impatient with them. After, she felt more mindful of the challenges they face, their strengths and limitations, and the ways in which they ascribe meaning to the events of their world.

These changed views of herself and the elderly had a profound impact on her troubled relationship with her family back in Ypsilanti, in particular with her seventy-year-old mother. "In my family you don't express anger or dissatisfaction," noted Judy. "My mother repeats to me that she never gets angry with her children. But I feel her anger through other things." For example, not long after the storm Judy learned of the serious car accident her sister had suffered. Judy decided that she would go to go home to Ypsilanti to see her. She hadn't been home for two years. When Judy called her mother to tell her that she would be arriving but that she would be staying with a brother and not her parents, her mother told her that she and her father might be too busy to see her when she came. Judy felt her mother's anger.

Yet Judy started to recognize that, like the elderly she had worked with at the shelter, her mother operated from a differ-ent context that Judy might now be better equipped to under-stand. While her mother had married and lived in the same place all her life, Judy, as she put it, "got rid of her husband" and moved far away to live on her own. But through it all, Judy said, "I had always beaten myself up for the problems that oc-curred between me and my mother." After the trauma of the shelter, however, Judy began to see things differently. First of all, Judy said, she had a better sense of her own self-worth. Be-fore she always felt bad that she wasn't "the perfect child." Second, Judy started to recognize that her mother's reactions didn't reveal faults in her but, instead, "revealed the lens through which she sees the world. This all sounds so simple, like I should have known this before. And the ice storm did not all of itself reveal this to me, but a lot of it jelled in the af-termath. I guess the experience broke through the normal routines that we fall into to get through the day and made me think about it."

In the months after the storm, every Tuesday afternoon in the supermarket Judy looked forward to running into two for-mer residents from the shelter. It was the elderly couple—the woman with Alzheimer's and her husband—that she had spent so much time with during the crisis. Whether or not the woman recognized her from week to week didn't matter. Judy was glad to see them.

A few days after power had been restored to our road I was home one morning trying to bring myself to resume preparing for the upcoming semester. At that time there were still large chunks of the north country without electricity and the word at Clarkson was that the semester's start would be pushed back by a week or more. Even so, I had little else to do but to get back at it. The trouble was that I had zero interest in doing so. The job seemed so distant to me. It was almost as if I had changed careers over the course of two weeks from teacher to home handyman—klutzy, semi-clueless, but coachable, and willing to learn new skills like adjusting the air-gas ratio in two-cycle engines.

Suddenly the power went out. I got up and looked out the window to see if there was evidence of power anywhere in sight. I got on the phone and started calling people. Power seemed to be out across the village. I was alive again. It was as if the power had left the grid and poured into me. I started to do a checkout of the house: the candles, flashlights, et cetera. I turned on the radio. Was it a story yet? I was smiling and excited. But I knew there was something perverse about that. "This is nuts," I told myself. "Calm down. It can't last."

It didn't, of course. About an hour later power was restored and the reality of prestorm living continued to loom over me. A week or so later I heard a weather forecaster predict that we might be getting hit by another ice storm. That day I also heard the panicky voice of a caller to North Country Public Radio who was clearly unnerved by the forecast. She said her husband was immobilized by fear of another ice storm. "We have to do something," she said, "to help each other handle all this." A wave of guilt washed over me. No one who lived through it—including myself—wants to live under those conditions. But why were so many of us so unsettled by the prospect of returning to the energized grid?

Late that afternoon, outside the door to Shirley and Lynn's house, I stood holding one of their gas cans that had found its way to my garage. I didn't just open the door and walk in. I knocked.

the grid and the village

n the end, as in all major disasters, the ice storm numbers were big. In the United States alone, the storm damaged about 18 million acres of rural and urban forests in Maine, New Hampshire, New York, and Vermont.[1] In New York the power outage lasted twenty-three days; more than 1,000 transmission towers were damaged; power companies replaced over 8,000 poles, 1,800 transformers, and 500 miles of wire.[2] In Canada the outage lasted thirty-three days; more than 1,300 steel towers were damaged; power companies replaced over 35,000 poles and 5,000 transformers.[3] The Canadian response involved the largest peacetime mobilization of military troops in the nation's history.[4]

The impact on the region's dairy herds was massive. In New York 1,400 out of 1,800 dairy farms in the storm region suffered losses; 1,200 out of 20,500 cows died, and 6,000 were rendered useless by mastitis.[5] In Canada 5,000 dairy farmers had to dump 13.5 million gallons of milk, and 27,000 dairy farms suffered damage to property and livestock costing more than 25 million Canadian dollars.[6]

All told there were at least seven hundred emergency shelters set up; 5 million people suffered power outages; at least thirty-five people were killed by storm-related house fires, falling ice, carbon-monoxide poisoning, and hypothermia.[7] The Worldwatch Institute reported that the cost of the damage on both sides of the border totaled $2.5 billion, about half of the cost of that inflicted by Hurricane Mitch ten months later.[8]

But the impact of the experience went beyond these quantifiable items. Consider for a moment one more statistic—one small, local, seemingly insignificant item: during the week in which the village of Potsdam was without any traffic signals or traffic control, only one minor fender-bender was reported.[9] Only one. Under normal circumstances accidents happen every day around here. Yes, Potsdam is a small town, but as in any active community, urban, suburban, or rural, there is just the right combination of traffic and tricky intersections to bring about a number of serious and sometimes fatal accidents. Now I realize that there were fewer cars on the road, thereby reducing the chance of an accident, but I drove through a few of the most dangerous intersections enough times in the early days of the event to know that there were plenty of chances for serious accidents to happen.

I think there was more going on than just fewer drivers on the road. I think drivers were more mindful of the act of driving during that experience. And it was this exercise in storm-induced mindfulness that may have the most lasting impact of the entire event.

When I use the term "mindful" I am thinking primarily about the qualities of thought elaborated by social psychologist Ellen J. Langer in her book *Mindfulness*.[10] (Like Langer, I realize that there is an ancient and rich discipline of mindfulness that arises out of Zen Buddhism. Although I am interested in that tradition, I do not claim to speak from within its practice.) As described by Langer, a mindful person is able to break out of the confines of conventional thinking and look at a situation or an event from different perspectives. Mindfulness comes from being open to new information and different ways of classifying it; mindful people recognize the larger contexts from which they derive meanings. So, for example, I might begin a journey to some sort of mindfulness when my mindless consumption of electric power is interrupted. If that change leads me to learn where electric power comes from, how it connects to my home, what can stop it from getting there, and what is required for me and my family to survive after losing our connection to the electric grid, I am becoming mindful about electric power. The changed environment might make me aware of new perspectives and new information, and give me an appreciation for the larger context of my actions, needs, and capabilities. It breaks me out of the routine, and if I educate myself to the implications of that broken routine, I can begin to increase my mindfulness. Yet increased mindfulness is not necessarily a pleasant or positive experience. Tragedy can induce a greater understanding of circumstances.

For people such as Martha Hartle, Judy Funston, Mitch Teich, Al Bradley, and me, the ice storm opened up a world of new information and how to classify it and made us mindful of facets of our pre- and poststorm lives. After the experience, Martha could put her career, her avocation—the EMT work—and her place in the local community into different, broader contexts. Many of the relations that connected Martha deeply to this place, a community she grew up in and where she has spent her entire life, had largely faded into the background of her daily routine. The storm blasted her out of that mindless practice. In contrast, Judy did not grow up here, and because she was largely unaware of local community life, she had developed few connections to it outside of her job. But as a result of her experience, she became more mindful of the needs and capabilities of others with whom she shares little but proximity. This change fed into her evolving relationship with

her family back in Michigan. As both Judy and Martha described, the storm-induced process of becoming mindful was a
jolting, gut-wrenching one. And the hard part for them and for
all of us who might have gained some mindfulness through the
storm was to carry that new perspective on after the power returned.

For Mitch Teich and his colleagues, perhaps they became
more mindful of the resourcefulness of their listeners and the
important connection those listeners have with the station. For
Al Bradley and his colleagues, perhaps they became more
mindful of the vulnerability of the infrastructures they build
and the resilience and patience of the customers they serve.

For me, I became more mindful of the richness and complexity of the connections between my family and the networks of support that helped my family withstand the crisis. In
other words, I became more mindful of the significance of the
several grids to which we are connected: the power grid, the
media and communications grids, and the social grid.

The Power Grid   Like most people, before the storm I
lived as if electricity came from light switches and power out-
lets. The storm changed that. And for me this book project became are exercise in further expanding my mindfulness about
electric power. It's as if I started to trace electricity back along
the lines from my house to the pole on the road to the local
substation to the transmission lines to one of the major sources
of that bulk power: the Moses-Saunders Power Dam twenty-
five miles away on the St. Lawrence. From there I could have
gone a number of places. I could have examined the environmental impact of the Seaway to illustrate the price we paid for
power. I could have explored in depth the growing worldwide
movement to oppose the building of large dams, most notably
the gargantuan Three Gorges project in China, as a way to
gauge power's costs. I could have followed the changes in the

power industry nationwide as state after state moves to deregulate its utilities. This movement toward a new free market for power could have led me to analyze the pros and cons of municipal power—the local, publicly owned and operated utilities that dot the nation—versus the massive corporate utilities that serve vast populations across the country. This issue has surfaced in New York; many communities like Potsdam are trying to decide whether or not to go into the public power business. Or perhaps I could have delved into the newly resurgent world of alternative energy sources, especially the recent advances in home power stations, which promise to further atomize the home by removing it from the power grid without sacrificing its electronic media connections.

I learned something about all of these issues in the aftermath of the storm, but I instead chose to explore a brief moment in time, noteworthy in historical terms but nearly forgotten nonetheless. The lost village of Louisville Landing is too small to merit mention in accounts of the dispossessed around the globe. For example, while McCully's *Silenced Rivers* provides a detailed accounting of the dispossession of lands by large dams and the forced relocation of millions of people worldwide, it does not mention the Seaway. But perhaps the case of Louisville Landing can serve as an example of the human costs of our reliance on electricity generated by ambitious undertakings like the Seaway.[11]

Yet while I want to argue that learning histories like that is part of the process of becoming mindful about electric power, I also want to reemphasize that my tale of the river from the first white surveyors to Robert Moses and the Seaway is a quintessential media construction. My version could serve as a treatment for the kind of documentary we might see on one of those ersatz "quality" cable channels, replete with commonly used if not hackneyed cinematic techniques like opening the story with a horrific crime and then putting off its resolution until the end, or filling the story out with fictionalized events in the lives of historic characters.[12] Furthermore, in addition to the interviews I conducted with some of the last residents of the submerged river communities, I used the work of several historians uncritically. I based key elements of my tale on research done by two Pulitzer Prize winners, Caro and Mabee, and one man, Franklin Hough, who was once known for pioneering the preservation of forests but is now largely forgotten.[13] So my tale is mediated by the representations of others who had their own agendas.

The Media and Communications Grids At the moment when I finally understood the extent of the storm, it certainly seemed as though my family and neighbors were cut off from the rest of the world. But this, of course, was never true. We were always able to get news about what was happening over the horizon thanks to two communication technologies that were only scarred, not killed, by the storm: radio and telephone. A number of regional radio stations were knocked out of service for a long time, but a few were able to come back and persist through the worst of it. Telephone service proved to be remarkably resilient. While segments of telephone customers lost service for some days, the primary cause of long-term telephone loss was the disabling of individual hookups, the service drops that were ripped off of houses by the ice buildup.

For me and my neighbors telephone connectivity was essential. Without it we most likely would not have gotten another generator beyond the original one that Lynn had the foresight to buy the day before the outage began. That loss alone might have been enough to put us in the shelter. Multiply that by thousands of people just in the area around Potsdam and combine it with the fact the Potsdam shelters were operating at full capacity and it is clear that telephone connectivity was essential. As we came to understand the amount of damage done to the power grid for hundreds of square miles, we came to appreciate phone service in ways we never had before.

If there had been no radio broadcasts to listen to, we most likely would have endured. But it is clear to me that while local radio might not have been essential, it provided profound support. It was a source for information, but it also became a virtual connection to others with whom we were sharing the experience. The psychological impact of this cannot be underestimated. To hear one another's stories; to know how others were handling events; to realize that others were having similar experiences; all of this mattered.

Other communication technologies were handicapped in a variety of ways. E-mail was seriously hampered throughout the region, primarily because generator power for the most part was insufficient to run the servers and clients necessary to sustain the networks. Both my home and work Internet services were unavailable until days after power was restored to both locations. Cable T.V. outages lasted in many places until well after electric power was restored. Withdrawal from T.V. became painful for many. A newspaper photo showed a large sign in front of one house saying, "Forget the power, we want our cable." There were also stories of people with wood heat running generators just to power T.V.s hooked up to home satellite dishes. Newspapers across the region were able to begin printing very limited editions by Saturday the tenth. In Montreal, the *Gazette* continued without interruption throughout the crisis.

When I look back at the range of newspaper articles that appeared during the crisis I see that many of them promoted standard disaster themes: fear, victimization, and mass sheltering. But overall it seems as though stories of social dissolution were outnumbered by stories of social cohesion.

Several types of stories communicated these messages.[14] The first were the fact-based stories about the storm and its effects, the classic five Ws type of journalism. Over time the news evolved, of course, from weather to power outages to relief services to recovery and its costs. Storm-related deaths were featured. While this type was part of a larger mix in the regional papers, it was the primary one that appeared outside of the disaster area. News of the ice storm did not start to appear in large urban newspapers across the nation until Saturday the tenth. And these stories were mostly wire service items that emphasized the breath of the storm, the number of people without power, the number and kinds of deaths, and statements from state and federal officials.

Another type of story focused on individuals coping with the storm conditions in a variety of situations. For example, in Montreal a number of stories examined life in the city's emergency shelters. In New York and Maine there were many accounts of the plight of dairy farmers, many of whom were fearful of losing their herds because their cows could not be milked without power, and cows that cannot be milked are in grave danger of disease and death.

The most compelling stories were those written to show how people's true natures were revealed by the storm. These were stories of helping, caring, and bonding across differences and conditions. A significant number of these illustrated the heroic and tireless efforts of the relief workers and utility crews. In addition, there were many glimpses of storm victims. A common theme in the victim stories set in urban areas was the breakdown of anonymity among people who lived near one another; in rural areas it was the innate hardiness of residents.

These images would solidify into the central theme of this diverse and complicated event—a theme that quickly became objectified and transformed into a standard narrative for news stories and a nice sales pitch for storm-related and not-so-related products. For example, over the months that followed the disaster, advertising for a whole range of consumer goods and services, from automobiles to flashlights and generators to wood-burning stoves to restaurants to bank accounts and investment plans, used that social-cohesion theme. These ads, combined with similar boilerplate synopses in news items, helped everyone learn that our true nature is that We All Pull Together in Times of Crisis.

This is not to say that during the disaster there weren't news stories emphasizing negative qualities brought out by the crisis. In Montreal, for example, it was mentioned that some people in shelters feared that their homes might be looted; other articles examined an increasing impatience with officials and tensions among storm victims as the crisis moved into its latter stages. In addition, on both sides of the border there were items about price gouging—opportunists who overcharged people for generators and other supplies—and the theft of generators. While both problems surfaced across the region, there seem to have been only a handful of cases documented.

The most common photos shown in print were the ones that illustrated the uniqueness of this particular disaster: apocalyptic views of crumbled transmission towers and beautiful images of the crystalline encasement of trees. These pictures accompanied national news stories in both countries. Within the storm region, those images were complemented by shots of people in shelters, especially ones where the residents looked unhappy or in distress.

While the bulk of the coverage focused on the immediate conditions, a small minority of stories tried to provide some context for the disaster, albeit in a limited way. After the first day or so articles began to appear, for example, that were intended to educate readers about the largely invisible technological systems that had failed. These were primers on the power grid, explaining how centralized power works, how it is transmitted and distributed, and how it is vulnerable. Another type of context was explored in some passing commentary that found its way into print. In English Canada there were some subtle but clear political statements about the nation's sovereignty issue. Some stories emphasized the fact that the Province of Quebec needed federal help and that federal help was unquestionably forthcoming. A few pieces pointed out that for those who already live disconnected from the grid—in northern New York, for example, there are a number of Amish farms—the storm was an inconvenience, not a crisis. This message was meant to emphasize how most people pay little attention to the infrastructure that supports our lives. On both sides of the border past accounts of catastrophic ice storms were recalled; in particular, storms that occurred after widespread electrification were recounted to illustrate how normal life was less disrupted by power outages decades in the past. Finally, there were some commentators who argued that the crisis was as much a technological failure as it was a weather-borne assault.

Overall, the standard issues were covered. The question is, does that breadth of coverage impose commonly held assumptions about disasters onto these particular events? If relatively few people actually experience disasters firsthand, perhaps media depictions of disasters foster common myths, most of which illustrate the negative consequences of the disaster events. These myths create expectations that are then repeatedly fulfilled by those who try to make sense of subsequent disasters.[15] Accordingly, while any one disaster may generate a diverse set of stories, those that have the most impact or that become featured are the ones that promote myths of social dissolution.[16] With the ice storm, as I noted above, national coverage emphasized the standard negatives: numbers of people killed, sheltered, and without power, and the estimated costs in dollars of the event. In contrast, local coverage promoted positive themes of social cohesion in addition to the standard negatives. These life-affirming images seem consistent with the findings of years of research that reveal how some communities pull together and social bonds become stronger under the adversity of natural disasters.[17] The urban neighborhoods and rural villages of the ice storm were becoming the "therapeutic communities" of natural disasters.

It is easy to become swept up by these manufactured representations of the "true nature" that is supposedly revealed in times of disaster. But how authentic are those messages about our natures? Aren't they just media constructions, patterns repeated over and over so that they become our own boilerplate explanations, our only language?

Perhaps I can illustrate this further by looking at similar events through yet another lens: in the documentary film *Six o'Clock News* there's a wonderful, telling sequence of events when filmmaker and narrator Ross McElwee trains his camera on an older couple helping to salvage their neighbor's belongings the day after a tornado had blasted through their Arizona trailer park.[18] We first see the couple as they display for McElwee's lens the family photos they were able to save for their neighbors. The photos were of the Sears Portrait Studio variety; posed, formal, ceremonial, almost monumental; the kind that show children or grandchildren as they should be but rarely are. By finding the framed pictures among the twisted chaos of aluminum, Formica, and pressboard paneling and by placing them in protective plastic, the neighbors had performed an essential task—saving memories, saving identities, saving the images we use to tell us who we are.

When Kath stood within our burning house and looked for the most important items to save, she chose wisely: she saved the baby pictures and the laptop computers, representations of family and the means to support that family. On the one hand, saving the pictures was something anyone might do in that situation; maybe it's what most people would do. On the other, for me it can't be reduced to a predictable, clichéd enactment of some social norm because it was simultaneously—paradoxically—a unique moment that defined something tenacious and caring about her and something indivisible about us. That moment is as powerful a memory as the thin line of flames snaking their way up our bedroom wall or the sound of the chain saw tearing into our roof. It's as if her instinctive, fleeting actions during the crisis burned into my mind the three of us bound together against the trauma of fire and destruction.

In McElwee's film we hear the narrator praise the woman for saving those pictures for her neighbor. But the story of the rescued pictures gets a bit more complicated when McElwee's camera pans across the wreckage to show a local T.V. news crew arriving to shoot the same events we've just experienced. And we begin to see the rescuers re-create the reality we thought we had just seen. Only now it seems less real. The first time the woman showed the pictures to McElwee's camera—our eyes—was the authentic moment, right?

McElwee lets us eavesdrop on the interview. The woman describes the tornado. It sounded like "a freight train," she says, but the T.V. camera operator is having a problem with the mike. Later she says it again for the camera, with real emphasis on "freight train." Hmmmm, this sounds familiar. The whole scene is familiar: trailer park, toilet seats and crushed velvet furniture scattered hither and yon, and a tornado that sounded like a freight train. Like the At Least We Saved the Baby Pictures story, this is the Tornado in the Trailer Park tale that gets told time after time in the news. And, accordingly, on this day even more news crews arrive for more retellings. Finally, McElwee shows her to us later that day as she watches herself appear on T.V. We hear one of the versions of her story. "That's me," she says.

There she was watching herself act out one of the roles we learn to play by watching tragedy on T.V. And here I am writing descriptions of a film about saving children's pictures in someone else's catastrophe as a means of better understanding my wife's act of saving our son's baby pictures in a catastrophe of our own. The levels of mediation between my son and my affection just keep stacking up.

In a review of *Six o'Clock News,* Robin Dougherty of the *Miami Herald* complained that McElwee didn't get inside the experience he purported to show us. "At times," Dougherty explained, "McElwee seems like the one person left on earth who hasn't experienced disaster firsthand. To anyone who has experienced the sort of events that he films, McElwee's position will seem to be that of someone on the outside looking in."[19] Perhaps, but for me that's just what McElwee's film is all about: the incredible difficulty of understanding that "firsthand" experience. It seems as though we are forever on the outside looking in *even when we are the insiders.*

It's that essential conflict with which we have to live: on the one hand our disaster experiences are unique and authentic while at the same time we learn that they follow patterns seen over and over again in disaster after disaster. If this is true, then the important realization is not that our experiences can be reduced to a set of common patterns or even myths, but that we're compelled to construct those patterns and myths. We need to characterize our experiences in ways we can understand. Whether we are touched by tragedy or survive intact, we need to objectify that experience somehow. Most of us do this by trading disaster stories with others. In doing that, we're processing our stories in terms of common themes and narratives. And natural disasters are perfect illustrations of this process: powerful geophysical forces happen and symbol-making, pattern-seeking, meaning-generating individuals interpret it. So our unique, authentic, indeterminate experience has to be somehow transformed and packaged by us into the symbolic and meaningful.

News coverage of disasters has been criticized as too often being formulaic and sensational, reducing complex events to graphic and emotional stereotypes.[20] Such coverage may be the result of a corporate efficiency that imposes its technique on selective events and churns out a repetitious product that best serves the corporate interest: attracting audiences to ads. But while I remain suspicious of the advertising ethic that drives all commercial media, my disaster experience has made me more mindful that the reductionism of news coverage isn't something that is done to us, it is something we participate in, given the opportunity. This is not a justification for lousy news coverage. It is not a celebration of the corporate media's unrelenting drive to induce more and more consumption. It is a recognition that news coverage, driven by corporate self-interest from start to finish, is one part of what makes us who we are.

Mitch at the radio station, for example, had been impressed by the way people seemed to want to call in and characterize their experiences in verse or reduce their essence to a *Life* magazine photo—but that's what we all do in one form or another. It serves as a kind of rough therapy that helps us grasp what we are going through. And because most of us usually experience these things only through mass media, we are most used to dealing with it on those terms. When we are faced with direct experience, we can better understand it if we can at least imagine what it would look like in some mediated story form, like in a magazine or on T.V. For good or ill, the disaster reveals our symbiotic relationship with our storytelling machineries. But this does not mean that we should sit back and passively consume whatever is served up to us.

Instead, it is crucial that we become or remain mindful of the here and now. If we lose sight of the local, then all we see is what is constructed for us, all we know is what is told to us via media sources. But if we can grapple mindfully with this place in this time—recognizing, of course, that that is not an unmediated act—we are striving for that authentic experience that the media critics and activists fear we've lost; we are attempting to have some control over our own imaginations. As hard as it might be, the mindful person tries to employ media images to his or her own ends.

This lesson extends to the ever evolving worlds of interactive media: the great hope of the Internet and the Web is that they empower individuals to participate actively in media communications. And certainly these infrastructures can serve local means quite significantly. But it should not be surprising that these vast interactive networks are increasingly seen as the means of delivering commercial content to a world of media consumers. The technology is not inherently participatory, but it clearly can enable individuals to employ media to their own ends *if they so choose.*

So perhaps an essential part of the disaster experience is to become part of a media event, even if it's just by proxy, as it is for most people. This doesn't mean, however, that we should happily accept the mass media status quo. We need to become more mindful of the box we are in with corporate media. We need to become more mindful of the increasing rates of consumption that are continually promoted by corporate media. Unbridled consumption is the most important environmental problem we face on a global scale. We need the critics, advocates, and activists who attempt to reveal this problem, who attempt to jam the media culture.[21] We need ever more sophisticated media literacies. But the mindful observer of media practices will see that it's not simply us versus them.

In an earlier chapter I wrote about the media critic who hesitated to agree that his perceptive analysis of the propagandistic practices of corporate media served as yet another form of entertainment for a particular audience of consumers—in other words, that his work was another media product, another propagandistic device. It is, of course. As is this book. What I think of as the prosocial advocacy of media critics is still a systematic effort to sway large segments of those critics' audiences. It is propaganda. And if it's well-done propaganda, like the best work of the media giants, then it's entertaining, too. There's no escaping it. Perhaps the only ethical out is to reveal our manipulative, propagandistic agendas as we employ them.

I am reminded that during the ice storm the local commercial radio stations became more like public radio, airing fewer ads and providing local and regional coverage as their main fare, while the public station became more like a commercial station by promoting the products that local businesses had to sell to help people endure the crisis. Both types of stations dispensed with their national syndications and as a result the media in our midst became vibrantly local.

In *The Wired Neighborhood* I argued that we should be wary of the globalizing force of new media technologies like the Internet. Instead, I said, people should invest those technologies in their local, geophysical place to improve the connectivity among those who share that place. But in retrospect, in considering responses to that argument, and certainly in light of my

ice storm experience, I realize that I had drawn a clear line between us, the community, and them, the communications
media, and the situation is more complicated than that. The
fact that two modern appliances of the communications
grid—telephone and radio—were essential to survival illustrates one small way that these media are fully embedded into
that amorphous thing I think of as my locality. For good or for
ill, local community is not merely the product of the interac-
tions among those with whom we share lives and location; it is
also a product of the corporate structuring of society. We are
local and national, national and global. We are individuals and
collectives. Mindfulness means that we understand that community is a grid and a village; it's both at once and each sepa-
rately. The media are not others; they are us.

The Social Grid   In a National Center for Atmospheric
Research editorial meant to undermine conventional thinking
about the impact of disasters on society, a provocative question
is posed: Is there an optimal number of disasters for any one
particular place?

> Given that a community experiences disasters (more
> precisely, hazardous events whether floods, hurricanes,
> earthquakes, etc.), over the long term there is an opti-
> mal number of disasters at which the community will
> experience the lowest societal costs (if, of course, they
> are able to incorporate the lessons of experience). In
> other words, if disasters occur too infrequently, the
> community will become complacent, let preparation
> atrophy, and face difficulties in addressing issues of
> long-term mitigation. If disasters occur too frequently,
> or a community is unable to incorporate the lessons of
> experience, then the community would likely be
> overwhelmed by the cumulative costs of the events.[22]

This line of thinking, on the one hand, is purely academic. We can do little or nothing to control those natural disasters listed, and even where it may be possible—flood control, for example—no sane community is going to say, Let's let the river flood us this year so we can be reminded of the lessons and remain prepared for the possibility that the water will rise over our current dikes.

Yet, in another way, this idea speaks directly to the concept of mindful living. The potential benefit of imagining an optimal number of disasters is the way it makes one think about preparedness. The starting point for vigilance is the recognition that disasters can happen and when they do, everything changes. It has to do with the shock, trauma, and insight that comes with what Kai Erikson calls the loss of our "immunity to misfortune," the realization that the systems and routines we rely on mindlessly are not absolute, permanent foundations but instead are vulnerable and finite.[23]

The vulnerability of crucial infrastructures became much publicized in the last years before the turn of the millennium, as we became aware of the Y2K computer problem. In hindsight, of course, we know that whatever potential there was for catastrophe, major problems were averted. But before the turnover to 2000, there was much speculation. And a comparison between the potential computer-based disaster and the 1998 ice storm was explicitly made by one publication, *Wired* magazine. In an article about the ice storm, Jacques Leslie provided a moving and perceptive recounting of the experience. But the editorial decision to use pictures of ice storm destruction and death—the crumbling transmission towers, the chaos of downed power poles and wires, broken forests, and stacks of dead, frozen cows—as a visual prediction of what would happen come the millennium was a classic case of shameless sensationalism.[24]

For others, the potential for Y2K destruction made them mindful of the potential social benefits of facing the challenge. In his *Utne Reader's Y2K Citizen's Action Guide,* published during the run-up to 2000, Eric Utne described a hopeful, life-affirming vision of the future in response to the possibility that the Y2K problem might undermine our electronic networks for a period of days or even weeks. The temporary loss of electronic connectivity was nothing to be feared, argued Utne. Instead, it was an opportunity to build authentic community. "As we prepare for Y2K, something surprising and unexpected and quite wonderful is going to happen. We're going to get to know our neighbors. Possibly for the first time in our lives, we will begin to know what it means to live in a real community. Most Americans these days live in networks, not communities. We tend to work, study and hang out with people who are like ourselves. We rarely associate with people who are not similar to us in terms of education, income, age, race, physical characteristics, and worldview. We put our old people in nursing homes and our young ones in day-care centers."

Utne's hope was that in the preparation for the temporary loss of the power grid and the electronic connectivities that come with it, we would have a means by which we'd become mindful of the social connections that bind together individuals who share place but not community. As Charles Halpern noted in the beginning of Utne's *Guide,* "This is a time for each of us not only to help our own local communities pull together but also to try to revive the idea of 'public citizenship.' By public citizenship I mean taking responsibility not only for the people who live close to us or who are our natural kindred spirits, but for those vulnerable and politically powerless people and countries who so often go 'unseen' and neglected. In this highly interdependent world we have created, their problems are, in fact, our problems."[25]

It is a bit unfair to compare this idea to the ice storm experience. After all, who would choose to live without heat, light, and water in order to experience a rebirth of community spirit? Even so, many of us have struggled with the fact that for those few weeks we became profoundly moved by the power of community ties. Yes, the local populations in the region—largely white, rural, middle class to poor—may be less diverse than in other regions. Still, many people in our community took responsibility for those who are "unseen" and vulnerable, in particular the elderly. But those actions served as a lifeline in what had to be a temporary situation. Perhaps for some of us it will open our eyes to the strengths of local life and the distractions of networked life. Perhaps it will open our eyes to the ways we waste power and time with empty consumption.

These are extremely important and clear lessons. Another lesson is less apparent but, I think, equally important: the trade-off for our electrified lives is the necessary trauma of knowing that we are inextricably bound to electricity and that its sources are inherently and forever vulnerable. That is, we choose to participate in a world dependent on electronic interconnections that can be interrupted by many forces. At the same time we know that we can be bound by social ties that comprise our community, connections that counter the trauma of forced interruption and provide some assurances against it. And maybe that's the best circumstance we can live under: a continual process of trauma and recovery.

As I have reconstructed it, the vast, complex series of events labeled "the ice storm" has been transformed into a fable of disaster-induced mindfulness for a number of people, myself included. But this kind of manipulation is open to the same charges commonly leveled at simplistic news coverage of disasters. News organizations are often accused of showing audiences only moments of high drama and destruction and then moving on to the next disaster. Such coverage offers little or no context with which viewers might come to some better understanding of the events under scrutiny. Likewise, it is overly simplistic for me to try to illustrate how individuals can become more mindful of crucial elements in their lives in light of a single experience like the ice storm. To me, for example, our house fire and the ice storm seem interrelated. Both events left my family vulnerable during the coldest time of the year and both highlighted for me the resilience of my family and the power of community ties. Even Judy Funston, who credited her ice storm experience with triggering insights into her relationship with her family and community, admitted that it wasn't just the ice storm that brought about those revelations. There was more to it than that. And for my neighbors Lynn and Shirley Warden, the difficulties of the ice storm were mere inconveniences compared to the magnitude of past traumas they have experienced. I began to realize this about them that night during the ice storm when Lynn and I sat at his kitchen table trading disaster stories.

He mentioned the tornado and Hurricane Agnes and I told him a bit about living near the Three Mile Island nuclear reactor during its partial core meltdown in 1979. But we were interrupted and the conversation was dropped. Some months later, when I began to formulate this book, I sat down with Lynn and Shirley to pick up that conversation.

As we started to talk, I was aware that they had been through a lot in their lives, but I was unprepared for where the conversation would go. In the end I understood that the source of their personal strength lay in their innate understanding of vulnerability and adversity and the ways that family and community provide assurances against those traumas.

Years ago, when Lynn was still living and working on his

father's farm near Corning in the southwestern part of New York State known as the Southern Tier, a tornado came through.

> It was a very eerie feeling. April, thundershowers, raining hard. We had completed the milking of the dairy herd that day, and it got black as the ace of spades, and you hear this noise and it was a warm night and the barn doors had been left open that night, and I told Dad, "I'm going to shut those doors." Coming back the noise was deafening. Dad yelled, "Let's head for the cellar." And we did. It came and went just like that. After it passed we come up and looked across the road. The barns were across the road. First thing we saw, one barn with no top to it at all. Second floor was gone. One large silo was twisted on the ground like a pretzel. These tornados, they just hop and skip, you know. Wherever the tail touches down. It came down the valley and up and over a hill a few miles. We just happened to be in its path.
>
> It didn't put my father out of business. Pick up the pieces and keep going. Those are the things you don't have any control over.

Some years later, after Lynn and Shirley were married, he was working in the fields at that same farm while a natural gas company truck was pumping gas out of a tank in the basement of the farmhouse. His parents had decided that they wanted to remove the tank from the house, but it still had gas in it, so the company had to pump it into a tank truck. While this operation was ongoing, unbeknownst to anyone, a coupling broke in the pump connection. Natural gas is heavier than air, so the escaping gas went down through an open cellar window and collected in the basement. Later Lynn's mother came home and went up to the second floor and at some point turned on a faucet. That engaged the water pump in the basement and the ignition from the pump sparked and lit up that pool of gas. The explosion blew a ball of fire out of the basement. Lynn's mother ran down the stairs and had to break a window to escape. The house didn't burn to the ground, but it took six months to rebuild. "I'd seen my parents go through a lot of adversity before and this was just another notch on the gun, so to speak. You see how your parents handle it and it affects the way you handle it."

In 1972 Lynn was a state trooper working out of a station near Corning and Shirley worked as a nurse in one of the hospitals when they both experienced the massive flooding caused by Hurricane Agnes. Although their home was not among those affected, their work put them in the heart of the disaster relief efforts.

The terrain there in Corning is lots of hills and valleys and the villages have dikes along the Chemung, which dumps into the Susquehanna, which eventually flows to Harrisburg. With all that rain, the water went over the dikes, which are as high as the second story of houses on the other side. The water filled the valley.

As a trooper, I worked to help flood victims. Started out patrolling in a boat. Went down through the center of Corning in an amphibious boat that we got from a fire department in Hammondsport, New York, a lake town. We were going on top of cars. Cars were under us. You could reach up and touch the stoplight. You had people up on the second story of buildings and your main concern was getting these people to high ground. Our first job was safety. Making sure everyone was out of it. Second was protection, make sure they weren't looted. Then later we'd help people get back in to survey the damage.

To this day I'm still amazed there were only three deaths. The devastation was extreme. It was muddy. You go down the street afterwards and everything in the house was thrown away. Couches, T.V.s, chairs. Everything was thrown into the street.

The most disheartening thing was the older people who lost everything they had. You'd see them, their biggest concern was finding the family Bible, knowing everything was gone. Those little things that meant so much to people, because the water ruined everything it touched. It really did. We sat and watched a house burn. Couldn't get to it. It was ironic, the water was up to about four feet around the sides. It burned down to that level.

Lynn's cousin's house floated off of its foundation and landed in the center of the road. Shirley's father and mother, who lived in Elmira, about fifteen miles up the Chemung, had about five feet of water in their house.

We didn't know where they were. We didn't have the communications like we had here with the ice storm. Telephone was wiped out. We went through some anxious moments trying to find them. Fortunately, with my job we were able to make some quick contact with the shelters they set up and about twenty-four hours later we found them. I'm sure a lot of people went through that, the same anxious moments. Families were separated. It was tough. People went from one fire station to another. Doctors couldn't find their patients after the flood. They had been delivered to one hospital or another.

You have to experience this kind of thing to understand it. I watch these things on T.V. and I can understand what these people are going through. Back during the flood I'd look at myself, whatever problems I might have, and I'd look at these people [in the flood] and say, "I don't have a problem."

In October of 1993, long after they had moved from Corning to Potsdam, Shirley was recuperating from a severe knee injury when they visited one of their daughters in the Albany area. On the drive home, Lynn started to experience some chest pains, but he kept driving.

Shirley couldn't drive. She had to sit in the backseat with her leg out straight. I felt bad, but you don't know it's a heart attack. How do you know what that feels like until you've had one? By the time we got to Potsdam and stopped for milk I said to Shirley, "This is bothering me bad now." And it hurt. I was pounding the steering wheel it hurt so bad. I said, "I got to get home and get some Maalox or something." We got home and she looked at me and said, "You're having a heart attack." I don't know how she knew, but being a nurse I guess she saw it.

She couldn't drive, so I said, "I'll drive to the hospital," but she wouldn't let me. The ambulance came and fortunately I got to the hospital, and they got me into the critical care unit and gave me this medicine, one of these miracle drugs that will thin the blood. It breaks the clot, but to be effective it has to be given in the first couple of hours. Which they did.

I thought I made it through that one. Then when I went to [the heart specialists in Burlington, Vermont] to get checked out, they did a catheterization and they said, "You need a triple bypass." That's when it hit home. Had the heart attack on October twelfth. Had the operation December fourth. Because the clot got broken up so soon there wasn't that much damage and I could wait for the surgery. Now my heart is as good as it ever was. I was fortunate there. I don't know if it was because of the other things I've been through, or what, but when they said that they strongly recommended heart surgery, I didn't bat an eye. I said, "Let's get it done. As soon as possible."

Three years later the car accident happened and all these events were put into perspective.

You find yourself trapped in an automobile accident, a guardrail over your leg, and you can't move. You're fifteen miles from nowhere. You look down, you're bleeding profusely, you know your leg is about cut off, you got a problem.

So when you've been faced with adversities and something comes along, you can say to yourself, "You don't have a problem here." You know what a real problem's all about. I can see where it would be very easy to throw up your hands and give up after things like these. But if a lot of things are working for you— you've got to have the support of family behind you, you've got to have the support of friends, you have to like what you're doing. I'm sitting here and there's never a time that you don't know it's gone. You get up in the morning and you get up with a leg and a half. Every morning you're reminded of it. It's not there. You grab a pair of crutches, you hobble into the bathroom, you take a shower on one leg. I can see where it would be very easy to say "The hell with it," you know what I'm saying? But you have the support. And sometimes you get angry to the point where you say "Hey, this is a challenge that's not going to get me down."

To say you don't get angry, that's a lie because you do get angry at times. Maybe that's good. Maybe that helps you get through it.

People say, "I don't know how a person can do it." Nobody knows until they're faced with it. People can do amazing things when they're faced with it. And they can go either way. I enjoy my work and it's not a problem to go to work in the morning.

If I didn't have all that, it might be pretty easy to dig a hole. Life is too short. There's still a lot of things I still enjoy in life and I intend to do them. It may not be the same as you knew it before but you learn to make your adjustments and live with it.

Then Lynn said something to me that I didn't anticipate. "I watched a son come through something. This isn't going to stop me."

"Son come through what?" I asked.

"Tommy was in kindergarten," said Shirley. "He got scarlet fever and then never got better after it. He was diagnosed with cancer on Lynn's mom's birthday, April 30. He was five years old." This began a regimen of continual trips to Syracuse for treatments.

We'd do his bone marrows early in the morning. We'd get up at 5 A.M. to drive to Syracuse to do them at eight so he could come back and do his sports in the afternoon so the kids in school didn't know he was sick.

I remember one day he was sure he was going to die. He was so sick. Seven years old and I was rocking him downstairs. His joints were huge. He was in a cast. He got a sore throat and his body just couldn't fight it, and he got damage to his knee from the infection. Lynn was feeling bad because he'd never talk to him about his fears. And I said to him, "Why don't you ever talk to Dad about it?" and he says, "Oh don't, because he'll cry."

"You know, you'll take a positive and you'll latch onto it," recalled Lynn. "We were down there and they told us that they treated a guy who is now the outstanding quarterback on his high school team. You say, 'Well, here's the positive to hold on to.'

"It was so important to keep normality. It was amazing to see how a child can adapt to this kind of thing and live with it. But it was very important for Shirley and me to keep it normal because it was very important to Tommy to not be different from anyone else. He didn't want people to think he was sick. We didn't coddle him. He played his baseball. He played his sports."

Shirley remembered when the family took a trip to Canton, Ohio, to see Bart Starr be inducted into the National Football League Hall of Fame. "His blood count was so bad that he almost should have been hospitalized. They had decided that he was so bad that it wouldn't make any difference so just make him happy. We never ate in restaurants, we ate along the road. He made it. He was all right.

"We saw another little boy not make it and you think, Is

mine not going to make it too? He went through a lot of ex-
perimental drugs. He went through one where I was giving
him a shot every four hours and he'd start throwing up at just
the thought of it because he knew that a half hour after the
shot he was going to start to throw up. One Saturday morning
I remember I called the doctor and said, 'This is it. I'm not
doing this to this kid anymore.' You know, we're trying to keep
his life normal and this is not normal."

Lynn remembered that Tom had a roommate in Syracuse
who didn't make it. "We got to the know the family, the parents of this girl who roomed with Tom. One day I go down to
relieve Shirley and she was gone."

The family went through twelve years of treatments with
him. Said Lynn, "He responded to chemotherapy, but there
was some tough going for some years. He had really rough
years in first and second grade. Very ill. Almost lost him twice.
We spent a lot of time in Syracuse and we went through a lot.
One of us was always in Syracuse and one of us was always here
working and taking care of the kids."

Shirley summed up the gravity of it all. "They told us we'd
never take him home."

"When I look back, he lived the kind of life you wanted
him to live," said Lynn. "Good student in school. Played his
hockey, played his football." Tommy went to college and grad-
uated with a degree in civil engineering. After graduation,
while working as a civil engineer in Syracuse, he started doing
volunteer work for sick kids in the community. Eventually, he
went back to school to become a physician's assistant, and now
he works at a major cancer treatment center in the Midwest.
"He told us, 'It's payback time,' " said Lynn. "We're proud of
him."

"When you face adversity like that, when a problem

comes along, you say, 'I haven't got a problem. No, I haven't got a problem.' "

When Kai Erikson studied people who had survived profound trauma, he wondered how it might change them: "What must it be like, having just discovered through bitter experience that reality is a thing of unrelenting danger, to have to look those dangers straight in the eye without blinders or filters?" [26] In response, Erikson offered one kind of answer to this question by describing how some people lose the ability to find any refuge from their fears. Danger might lurk just out of sight or it might suddenly descend upon them, but it was always present. Everything they experienced became poisoned because the trauma had stripped away any sense of protection.

But in Lynn and Shirley's stories, like those of others in this book who weathered great catastrophes, we see a remarkable resilience. For Lynn and Shirley protection is bound up with family and community. For the first settlers down on the St. Lawrence, the pioneers who carved out of the dense forests a grid of civilization as a hedge against their enemies, family and community were their primary protections from the dangers of winter, wilderness, and war. For the victims of the ice storm two hundred years later, suddenly cut off from the protections of the power and communications grids, family and community became the primary defense against the dangers of winter and isolation. And by the time they returned to the safety of the electrified grids, they had come to realize that there existed in that place at that time a web of support that many people thought had long since withered away from disuse.

At the end of a public-radio retrospective of the ice storm, Ellen Rocco, the manager of North Country Public Radio, summed up the lesson of her experience:

For that critical first week it was family, friends, and neighbors doing for each other. Not unlike the experience of a funeral, or wedding, or family crisis, the rest of the world seemed distant and irrelevant. When I listened to the radio or was at the station reading a newscast, it was the shelter phone number or free wood pickup location or instructions for draining water pipes or information about signaling rescue helicopters that mattered. It was the north country that mattered. Period.

We all have our snapshot and audio memories: the ice wrapped half an inch thick around branches and bending full-grown trees to the ground, the sharp crack of those trees giving way to their crystal burden; the eerie scene of unlit towns; streets and roads crisscrossed by wires, poles, and tree limbs; the stillness, the isolation. But this is what I'll tell my grandchildren: that we took care of each other. We didn't wait for a faraway, anonymous agency to pick up the pieces. Family, friends, neighbors, community, we took care of each other. Perhaps imperfectly, but unforgettably well.[27]

afterword a disaster timeline

January 1 to 4, 1998

A high-pressure ridge builds along the East Coast. An air current circulating around the ridge brings warm, moist air from the Gulf of Mexico inland across the Gulf Coast. Meanwhile, the polar jet stream moves southward and extends deep into the Southeast before turning northward to the East Coast. The warm, moisture-laden air from the gulf is squeezed between the high-pressure system and the colder northern air and a powerful rain-producing storm begins to move up the coast.[1] For a few days the storm stretches from the Gulf coast to the northeast.

January 5

- Homes are flooded near New Orleans, Louisiana, as eight inches of rain falls in twenty-four hours.[2]
- Surface icing starts to build in parts of the northeastern United States and eastern Canada.
- Power outages begin to appear in Quebec.
- Schools are closed across northern New York.
- Judy Funston travels to jury duty.

January 6

- The National Weather Service issues a flash flood watch across southern Arkansas; the Arkansas River approaches flood stage.[3]
- The storm continues to bring ice across the northeast.
- Officials begin setting up emergency shelters in eastern Canada.
- Al Bradley is called out to work the storm with the line crews.

January 7

- Sixty-mile-an-hour winds trip off tornado sirens in the middle of the night at Catawba (South Carolina) Nuclear Station. Flash flood watches are posted for Charlotte, North Carolina.[4]
- As six inches of rain falls on Shelby County, Alabama, a five-year-old girl is swept away and drowns. A sixty-two-year-old woman drowns after falling from a footbridge into a swollen creek. In Tennessee two people are confirmed dead in flooding. At a church cemetery in Hattiesburg, Mississippi, coffins float to the surface as the ground becomes saturated by the unrelenting downpour.[5]
- Across central New York State rivers and streams in many low-lying areas begin to flood. Icing persists in the northeast.
- The number of power outages continues to rise from New York to Maine and across eastern Ontario and southern Quebec.
- Lynn Warden buys a generator and travels home from Syracuse.
- Officials from the town and village of Potsdam begin to discuss emergency response plans.

January 8

- The ice storm intensifies across the region.
- In Canada six deaths are attributed to the storm and over one hundred people are treated for carbon monoxide poisoning caused by the indoor burning of fossil fuels to cook and keep warm.[6]
- More than four hundred thousand households in the Montreal region are without power for a second day.[7]
- The power grid in northern New York goes dead and Niagara Mohawk Power sets up a storm response command post in Syracuse.
- New York governor George Pataki declares a state of emergency in the five northernmost counties.
- In Potsdam, local officials establish an emergency shelter on the SUNY campus and the first refugees arrive. Martha Hartle discovers that she is in charge of the shelter's medical section.
- Across northern New York radio stations are out of service. Mitch Teich and his colleagues at North Country Public Radio struggle to get the station back on the air.
- Marge Howe takes care of her friend Hubie as his oxygen supply is threatened.

January 9

- The ice continues to build. The city of Montreal goes dark. The death toll in Canada rises to ten.[8] Two and half million people in Quebec are without power.
- In Maine, more than two hundred thousand calls for help are made to Central Maine Power as outages spread.
- Parts of Vermont and New Hampshire are declared disaster areas by state officials.
- In New York a ban on all nonemergency travel is instituted.

- Martha Hartle and her colleagues begin to organize the medical wing of the shelter.
- Oxygen is finally procured for Marge Howe's friend Hubie.
- Judy Funston moves into her office on the SUNY campus and volunteers to help at the shelter.
- Mike Warden and Dave Centofanti search for gasoline.
- Lynn and colleagues open a local drugstore to sell supplies.
- My neighbors and my family begin pooling our resources at the Wardens' house.

January 10

- The death toll from flooding in northeastern Tennessee reaches seven; dozens are reported missing.[9]
- In Florida, the *Fort Lauderdale Sun-Sentinel* reports that the storm has caused nineteen deaths from the southern plains to the northeast.[10]
- The mayor of Montreal, Pierre Bourque, states that the storm is causing "an enormous ecological disaster for all the vegetation in the city."[11]
- In the Montreal region more than thirty power distribution towers fall during the day, while the number of emergency shelters across the province increases to two hundred.[12]
- In New York, as the storm begins to dissipate, Governor Pataki orders the National Guard and other state emergency response agencies to aid in the disaster response.[13]
- In Potsdam, local physicians reach the emergency shelter and begin seeing patients housed there.
- Gasoline supplies at Potsdam gas stations are held for emergency use by rescue vehicles.
- My in-laws defy the travel ban and deliver a generator and a supply of gas.
- Several of us get to the darkened supermarket and buy supplies.

- North Country Public Radio opens its phone lines so that locals can call to speak on air.

January 11

- President Clinton declares a federal state of emergency in the five counties of northern New York.
- Across parts of Vermont, New Hampshire, and Maine over 260,000 homes and businesses are without power. Carbon monoxide poisonings are reported across the region.[14]
- At least twenty-five thousand phone lines are down across northern New York.[15]
- In Quebec more than three million people are without power. The number of shelter residents in the province more than doubles from Friday the ninth to Sunday the eleventh.[16]
- In New York more than 120 shelters are open.[17]
- The Potsdam shelter is operating at near capacity. A variety of Sunday church services are held there.
- Before dawn Marge Warden's water breaks and she checks in to the hospital.
- A medical unit from the New York National Guard arrives at the shelter.
- The daytime high temperature in the region drops to well below freezing.
- Potsdam officials decide not to stop citizens who are traveling the area looking for survival supplies.
- Our generator stops running at night as the temperature drops below zero degrees.
- Public radio opens its phone lines all evening long.
- Marge Warden has a baby boy.

January 12

- The death toll from the southeastern United States to Canada rises to twenty-four.

- National Guard helicopters patrolling a seven-thousand-square-mile area of northern New York rescue sixteen people trapped in isolation.[18]
- The Ontario Provincial Police report that fifty-one electric generators have been stolen in a number of separate incidents across eastern Ontario near the Quebec border.[19]
- More than 1,500 dairy farmers in Ontario request industrial-sized generators to help them maintain their herds.[20]
- Downtown Montreal remains without power.
- Lynn's generator dies—he travels to Syracuse and returns with two others. The rest of us eat at the Clarkson shelter.

January 13

- Thousands of relief workers and millions of dollars of supplies flow into affected regions.[21]
- Utility crews from across the nation continue to arrive, one from as far away as Hawaii.[22]
- The *Montreal Gazette* publishes a list of more than eighty rural municipalities that cannot expect to be returned to the power grid for another seven to fourteen days.[23]
- Quebec hospitals operate at full capacity.[24]
- In Potsdam, the hospital's emergency room handles double its normal volume of patients.
- In the evening power is restored to the houses on my road. Our neighbors across the road, Dave and Cindy, are still without power because their service drop has been torn off the house.
- Power remains out in 70 percent of St. Lawrence County.

January 15 to February 8

The dangers and recovery continue. On January 15 the death toll in Quebec rises to fifteen when a farmer riding his tractor is decapitated as a power line snaps and whips down on him.

On that same day downtown Montreal businesses are able to open for the first time, Niagara Mohawk installs a large generator at North Country Public Radio to power all station operations, and Dave and Cindy's electricity is restored. On January 18 Judy Funston's house gets power. The shelters across northern New York begin to close during the final week of January. The power grid in New York is fully restored by January 30. In Quebec the grid is fully restored by February 8, more than a month after the storm first hit.

one from accidents to disaster

1. For a textbook analysis of media literacy see W. James Potter, *Media Literacy* (Thousand Oaks, Calif.: Sage, 1998). For a sampling of related critical and historical perspectives see Dean Alger, *Megamedia* (Lanham, Md.: Rowman and Littlefield, 1998); Susan Douglas, *Inventing American Broadcasting 1899–1922* (Baltimore Md.: Johns Hopkins University Press, 1997), and *Listening In: Radio and the American Imagination* (New York: Times Books, 1999); Stuart Ewen, *All Consuming Images* (New York: Basic, 1988), and *PR!* (New York: Basic, 1998); Thomas Frank, *The Conquest of Cool* (Chicago: University of Chicago Press, 1997); Robert McChesney, *Telecommunications, Mass Media, and Democracy: The Battle for the Control of U.S. Broadcasting, 1928–1935* (New York: Oxford University Press, 1995), and *Rich Media, Poor Democracy* (Champaign: Univ. of Illinois Press, 1999); Bill McKibben, *The Age of Missing Information* (New York: Plume, 1993); Mark Crispin Miller, *Boxed In: The Culture of TV* (Evanston, Ill.: Northwestern University Press, 1988); Neil Postman, *Amusing Ourselves to Death: Public Discourse in an Age of Show Business* (New York: Penguin, 1985); Leslie Savan, *The Sponsored Life* (Philadelphia: Temple University Press, 1994); Danny Schecter, *The More You Watch, the Less You Know* (New York: Seven Stories, 1997); Herbert I. Schiller, *Culture, Inc.* (New York: Oxford University Press, 1989); Norman Solomon, *The Habits of Highly Deceptive Media* (Monroe, Me.: Common Courage, 1999).

two origins of a grid, part 1

1. David E. Nye, *Electrifying America: Social Meanings of a New Technology, 1880–1940* (Cambridge: MIT Press, 1990), 26.

2. Nye, *Electrifying America,* 22.

3. Nye, *Electrifying America,* 384. His biography in this book said he taught at the University of Copenhagen. A more recent book indicated he taught at Odense University.

4. Franklin B. Hough, *A History of St. Lawrence and Franklin Counties* (Albany: Little and Company, 1853), 335. Chapter Two is based on the stories recounted in Hough's history, which is the earliest comprehensive history of Macomb's Great Purchase and all of the towns and events that followed.

5. Hough, *History,* 262–265.

6. For an overview of the events in and around New York state leading up to the War of 1812, see James Sullivan, ed., *History of New York State 1523–1927,* vol. 3 (New York: Lewis Historical Publishing Co., 1927), 1071–1123.

7. For a description of what it was like to clear wilderness and create farms in rural New York state see D. Ellis, J. A. Frost, H. C. Syrett, and H. J. Carman, *A History of New York State* (Ithaca: Cornell University Press, 1967), 163–172.

8. Harry F. Landon, *The North Country: A History Embracing Jefferson, St. Lawrence, Oswego, Lewis and Franklin Counties, New York,* vol. 1 (Indianapolis: Historical Publishing, 1932), 87–93.

9. Ellis et al., *History,* 150–162. See also Landon, *North Country,* 128.

10. For a comprehensive analysis of the history of the political struggles to change the river from 1700 up to the 1950s see William R. Willoughby, *The St. Lawrence Waterway: A Study in Politics and Diplomacy* (Madison: University of Wisconsin Press, 1961).

11. Hough, *History,* 620.

12. Hough, *History,* 642.

13. For a firsthand account of a man, Zaddock Steele, who was taken into two years of captivity during this raid, see "The Captivity of Zaddock Steele," in Colin G. Calloway, ed., *North Country Captives: Selected Narratives of Indian Captivity from Vermont and New Hampshire* (Hanover, N.H.: University Press of New England, 1992), 100–149.

14. For a discussion of the difficulty of travel across this frontier during the

first decade of the nineteenth century see Landon, *North Country*, 116–125.

15. Hough, *History*, 263.

16. For a detailed analysis of the role that the building of roads and canals played in the dispossession of Iroquois land across western New York, see Laurence M. Hauptman, *Conspiracy of Interests: Iroquois Dispossession and the Rise of New York State* (Syracuse: Syracuse University Press, 1999).

17. Frank Graham, *The Adirondack Park: A Political History* (Syracuse: Syracuse University Press, 1978), 10.

18. This Jacob Brown, a highly successful smuggler of potash and other valuable materials during the years when trade between the United States and Great Britain was banned, was the same Jacob Brown—General Brown—who later became a celebrated military commander during the War of 1812. See Patrick A. Wilder, *The Battle of Sackett's Harbour, 1813* (Baltimore: Nautical and Aviation Publishing Company of America, 1994), 1–7.

19. Hough, *History*, 337.

20. Hough, *History*, 334. In addition to this excerpt, Hough's presentation of the story of the four men includes the story of the daughter of one of them who had a premonition of danger. Hough does not say which man's daughter it was. Nor does he discuss the lives of these men as I have. Those details are drawn from accounts of contemporaries appearing in the sources I cite.

21. This excerpt is from an early-twentieth-century translation of Handsome Lake's code by William Bluesky from a recitation by Edward Cornplanter, a Seneca follower of Handsome Lake. It is included here as it is presented in Robert W. Venables, introduction to *The Six Nations of New York: The 1892 United States Extra Census Bulletin* (Ithaca: Cornell University Press, 1995), xiii.

three the grid crumbles

1. The transcript was archived at http://www.tv.cbc.ca/national/pgminfo/trans/T980108.html.

four origins of a grid, part 2

1. Much of the reconstruction of life on the river from the 1920s to the 1950s came from interviews conducted by Dalton Foster and myself with

people who lived on the river in those years. These interviewees included Roy Barstow, Carleton Dignean, Frieda Dignean, Ray Lancto, Ersel Logan, Stan Logan, and Bill Spriggs. In addition, I was graciously allowed to use a videotape of interviews with Bill Bartlett, Harold Griffith, and Win Veetch, who were interviewed by Curt Robinson and Roger Waters for a local history project about life on the river before the Seaway.

2. See the map of the St. Lawrence projects in Williams R. Willoughby, *The St. Lawrence Waterway: A Study in Politics and Diplomacy* (Madison: University of Wisconsin Press, 1961), 176–177.

3. A variety of historical details about Louisville Landing were reported locally in the years leading up to World War II in "First Louisville Landing Customs House Being Razed After Standing 150 Years," *Massena Observer*, 21 August 1938; "Early Customs House at Louisville Landing Razed," *Massena Observer*, 24 August 1939; "North Village to be Inundated by Seaway," *Massena Observer*, 21 June 1941.

4. "Landmarks to Vanish in Wake of Projects," *Massena Observer*, 30 March 1955.

5. "67 Year-Old Croil Islander Shoots Long Sault Rapids Safely in Homemade Boat," *Massena Observer*, 7 October 1941.

6. "Lehman Advances Program to Help Business in State," *New York Times*, 15 January 1941.

7. "Text of Governor Lehman's Message Submitting the Budget to the Legislature," *New York Times*, 27 January 1942.

8. Robert A. Caro, *The Power Broker: Robert Moses and the Fall of New York* (New York: Knopf, 1974).

9. Robert Moses, *Public Works: A Dangerous Trade* (New York: McGraw-Hill, 1970), 355–356.

10. Robert Moses, *Land Acquisition on the American Side for the St. Lawrence Seaway and Power Projects*, New York Power Authority booklet, 18 July 1955, 1.

11. Howard G. Barrow, "Seaway Great—But, Declare Louisvillians Due to Yield Homes," *Watertown Times*, 6 August 1954.

12. Carleton Mabee, *The Seaway Story* (New York: Macmillan, 1961), 291.

13. Mabee, *Seaway Story*, 214.

14. Willoughby, *St. Lawrence Waterway*.

15. Lowell Thomas, *Lowell Thomas' Story of the St. Lawrence* (New York: Henry Stewart, 1957), 20. Two other histories discuss the Canadian reloca-

tion only: Lionel Cheurier, *The St. Lawrence Seaway* (New York: St. Martin's, 1959), and T. L. Hills, *The St. Lawrence Seaway* (New York: Praeger, 1959).

16. Andrew H. Brown, "New St. Lawrence Seaway Opens the Great Lakes to the World," *National Geographic* 115, no. 3, 324.

17. Clara Ingram Judson, *St. Lawrence Seaway* (Chicago: Follett, 1959).

18. John H. Brior, *Taming of the Sault* (Watertown, N.Y.: Hungerford-Holbrook, 1960), 40.

19. Laurence Hauptman, *The Iroquois Struggle for Survival: World War II to Red Power* (Syracuse: Syracuse University Press, 1986).

20. Caro, *Power Broker,* 708–709.

21. Moses, *Public Works,* 880.

22. Dan Henry, "The St. Lawrence Seaway Before and After," available from the Massena Public Library, Massena, N.Y.

23. Mabee, *Seaway Story,* 201.

24. Mabee, *Seaway Story,* 201.

25. "Seaway Statistics in Men, Cubic Yards, and Dollars," *Toronto Star Weekly,* 27 June 1959.

26. Mabee, *Seaway Story,* 182.

27. From an interview with Bill Spriggs, the foreman, conducted by Dalton Foster and me.

28. David Stout, "U.S. Sues 7 Utilities on Air Pollution Charges, Citing 32 Coal-Fired Plants in 10 States," *New York Times,* 4 November 1999.

29. Richard Perez-Pena, "Power System Use Is Pressing Limits in New York Area," *New York Times,* 9 July 1999.

30. Jim Abrams, "Plan Proposed to Reduce Blackouts," Associated Press, 19 June 1999.

31. David M. Herszenhorn, "Ever-Surging Demand for Electricity Is Posing Summer Challenge for Utilities," *New York Times,* 28 June 2000; William Booth, "Mutiny on the Meter?" *Washington Post,* 3 December 2000; Nancy Rivera Brooks and Nancy Vogel, "State Declares First Stage 3 Power Alert," *Los Angeles Times,* 8 December 2000.

32. For example, Andrew Murr, "A River Runs Through It," *Newsweek,* 12 July 1999, 46.

33. Patrick McCully, *Silenced Rivers: The Ecology and Politics of Large Dams* (Atlantic Highlands, N.J.: Zed, 1996), 308.

34. Mabee; *Seaway Story,* 220.

five the grid rebuilt

1. Mark Abley, *The Ice Storm* (Toronto: McClelland and Stewart, 1998), 176.

six the grid and the village

1. Federal Emergency Management Agency (FEMA), "January 1998 New York Ice Storm," Region II report, http://www.fema.gov/reg-ii/1998/nyice2.htm.
2. Jim Murphy, "NiMo Recaps Ice Storm," *Daily Courier-Observer* (Potsdam-Massena, N.Y.), 10 March 1998.
3. Mark Abley, *The Ice Storm* (Toronto: McClelland & Stewart, 1998), 14–27.
4. Michael Parfit, "Living with Natural Hazards," *National Geographic* 194, no. 1 (July 1998), 12.
5. FEMA, "Ice Storm."
6. Abley, *Ice Storm.*
7. Abley reports well over 539 shelters in Quebec and Ontario. A conservative estimate would add at least another couple of hundred across the rest of the affected region. Published reports of the number of killed vary, although thirty-five seems to be the most common estimate. The reported death toll is forty-five in Jacques Leslie, "Powerless," *Wired* 7, no. 4 (April 1999), 120.
8. Janet N. Abramovitz and Seth Dunn, "Record Year for Weather-Related Disasters," Vital Signs Brief 98-5, Worldwatch Institute, 27 November 1998, http://www.worldwatch.org/alerts/981127.html. As with the number of deaths, this figure varies from report to report. The Worldwatch number is the highest and the most recent of the figures I found.
9. I should note here that in an interview with the village police chief, he said there had been no accidents during that time period. It was in an interview with the village administrator that I was told that one of the relief officials had been involved in a minor accident.
10. Ellen J. Langer, *Mindfulness* (Reading, Mass.: Addison-Wesley, 1989).
11. Patrick McCully, *Silenced Rivers: The Ecology and Politics of Large Dams* (Atlantic Highlands, N.J.: Zed, 1996).
12. Hough's account tells us only the last names of the four Americans and the story of the fatal crossing, the dog, and the premonition of the daughter of one of the party.

13. Hough wrote several histories, but he achieved the greatest prominence as the first head of the U.S. Division of Forestry in 1881. See, for example, Robin L. Pinto, "A History of the Wilderness Concept and the Efforts Toward Its Preservation: Influences of Frederick Law Olmsted, Arthur Carhart and Aldo Leopold," a Paper Presented in Recreation Dimensions of Natural Resource Management, 28 August 1988, http://nexus.srnr. arizona.edu/~gimblett/wild4.html.

14. Many of these stories are still available through the online archives services of the *Montreal Gazette,* at www.montrealgazette.com, and the *Ottawa Citizen,* at www.ottawacitizen.com.

15. Russell R. Dynes, "The Impact of Disaster on the Public and Their Expectations," University of Delaware Disaster Research Center, preliminary paper no. 234, 1995.

16. Dennis Wenger and Barbara Friedman, "Local and National Media Coverage of Disaster: A Content Analysis of the Print Media's Treatment of Disaster Myths," University of Delaware Disaster Research Center, article no. 185a, 1986; first published in *International Journal of Mass Emergencies and Disasters* 4 (1986), 27–50. See also E. L. Quarantelli, "Local Mass Media Operations in Disasters in the USA," University of Delaware Disaster Research Center, article no. 300, 1996; first published in *Disaster Prevention and Management* 5 (1996), 5–10.

17. Kai Erikson, *A New Species of Trouble: The Human Experience of Modern Disasters* (New York: Norton, 1994), 236.

18. Ross McElwee, *Six o'Clock News,* First Run Features, New York. Originally aired on *Frontline,* 21 January 1997. See http://www.pbs.org/wgbh/pages/frontline/shows/news/.

19. For a collection of press reactions to the film, see http://www.pbs.org/wgbh/pages/frontline/shows/news/etc/reactions.html.

20. Susan D. Moeller, *Compassion Fatigue: How the Media Sell Disease, Famine, War, and Death* (New York: Routledge, 1999), 53, 313–322.

21. For perhaps the best illustration of this activism see the work of Kalle Lasn and his colleagues in their *Adbusters* magazine at www.adbusters.org. See also Kalle Lasn, *Culture Jam: The Uncooling of America* (New York: William Morrow, 1999).

22. Roger A. Pielke, "An Optimal Number of Disasters?" *Weather Zine* 12 (October 1998), University Corporation for Atmospheric Research, www.dir.ucar.edu/esig/socasp.

23. Erikson, *New Species of Trouble,* 152.

24. Leslie, "Powerless."

25. Charles Halpern, "Foreword," *Utne Reader's Y2K Citizen's Action Guide* (Minneapolis: Utne Reader Books, 1998), 11. Also available at www.utne.com/y2k.

26. Erikson, *New Species of Trouble,* 153.

27. Ellen Rocco, "One Year Later: Commentary by Ellen Rocco," *Ice Storm '98: A Retrospective,* North Country Public Radio audio cd, www.ncpr.org, 1999.

afterword a disaster timeline

1. Dante Ramos, "Residents Finally Get a Chance to Dry Out," *New Orleans Times-Picayune,* 8 January 1998.

2. Natalie Pompilio and Dante Ramos, "Jeff Put on Alert for More Flooding," *New Orleans Times-Picayune,* 7 January 1998.

3. Noel E. Oman, "Storms Leave 2,300 Homes in Dark," *Arkansas Democrat-Gazette,* 7 January 1998.

4. "Tornado Sirens Activated during Overnight Storm," *The Rock Hill (S.C.) Herald,* 8 January 1998.

5. Mike Morris, "Southeast Storms Kill at Least Four," *Atlanta Journal-Constitution,* 8 January 1998.

6. *The National,* transcripts online at http://www.tv.cbc.ca/national/pgminfo/trans/T980108.html.

7. Susan Semenak, "Coming in from the Cold," *Montreal Gazette,* 8 January 1998.

8. *The National,* transcripts online at http://www.tv.cbc.ca/national/pgminfo/trans/T980109.html.

9. "Ice Storm Slams Northeast," *Tampa Tribune,* 10 January 1998.

10. "An Icy Mess," *Fort Lauderdale Sun-Sentinel,* 10 January 1998.

11. Philip Authier, "Ecological Disaster: Bourque," *Montreal Gazette,* 10 January 1998.

12. Jonathon Gatehouse et al., "From Bad to Worse," *Montreal Gazette,* 10 January 1998.

13. Raymond Hernandez, "National Guard Is Sent to Aid Ice Storm Victims Upstate," *New York Times,* 10 January 1998.

14. "Northeast Is Cold, Dark in Storm's Wake," *Los Angeles Times,* 11 January 1998.

15. "An Ice-Bound Region Struggles to Recover," *New York Times,* 12 January 1998.

16. Lynn Moore, "Crowded Shelters Beginning to Show Evidence of Strain," *Montreal Gazette,* 11 January 1998.

17. "Northeast Is Cold, Dark in Storm's Wake," *Los Angeles Times,* 11 January 1998.

18. "National Guard Looks for Stranded People," *St. Louis Post-Dispatch,* 12 January 1998.

19. Zachary Houle, "Generator Thieves Packing Heat," *Ottawa Citizen,* 12 January 1998.

20. Andrew McIntosh, "Region Struggles to Its Feet," *Ottawa Citizen,* 12 January 1998.

21. Frank Brieaddy, "Kitchen, Foodstuffs Head North for Relief," *Syracuse Post Standard,* 13 January 1998.

22. "Hawaiian Utility Workers Help Restore Power in Icy Northeast," *Washington Post,* 13 January 1998.

23. "Rural Towns Wait, Hope," *Montreal Gazette,* 10 January 1998.

24. Jeff Heinrich and Cheryl Cornacchia, "Hospitals Bursting at the Seams," *Montreal Gazette,* 13 January 1998.

index

207